THE LANCASHIRE BIBLIOGRAPHY

PART ONE : DIRECTORIES

LANCASHIRE
DIRECTORIES
1684-1957

Compiled by

G. H. TUPLING, M.A., B.Sc., Ph.D.

Revised, enlarged and edited by

SIDNEY HORROCKS, F.L.A.

MANCHESTER

JOINT COMMITTEE ON THE LANCASHIRE BIBLIOGRAPHY

1968

©

1968

Published by

THE JOINT COMMITTEE ON THE LANCASHIRE BIBLIOGRAPHY

CENTRAL LIBRARY, MANCHESTER 2

Printed by

RICHARD BATES LIMITED, SOUTHMOOR ROAD,

WYTHENSHAWE, MANCHESTER 23

FOREWORD

The Joint Committee on the Lancashire Bibliography was set up in 1950 with the task of compiling a bibliography of printed material relating to Lancashire. The Committee comprises representatives of the Community Council of Lancashire, the North Western Branch of the Library Association, the North Western Regional Library System, the Lancashire Record Office, Manchester City Libraries, and the Lancashire Urban District Councils Association. The work on the Bibliography has been financed by grants from local authorities, the Universities of Manchester and Liverpool, the Community Council, industrial and commercial firms, and local history societies. Until 1962 the Bibliography was under the editorship of Dr. G. H. Tupling, a distinguished local historian who for many years was Special Lecturer in Local History at the University of Manchester. On Dr. Tupling's death late in 1962, he was succeeded as Editor in October, 1963 by Mr. Sidney Horrocks, who had been Chief Assistant Librarian (Reference Libraries) of the Manchester City Libraries and who was well known for his bibliographical work.

The Lancashire Bibliography covers material printed up to the end of 1957, and at present consists of more than 70,000 items maintained in a card catalogue in the Bibliography Office at the Manchester Central Library. The work of editing is not yet complete, but some sections of the Bibliography are either ready or almost ready for publication. It is proposed to start publishing these sections now, beginning with this list of Directories. Directories form a natural starting point for much research into local history during the eighteenth and nineteenth centuries.

They are a valuable source for urban history, but one which has been somewhat neglected. This neglect may arise from the fact that early directories are among the rarest of books and are not always easy to locate. The list here printed shows what directories are available in Lancashire Libraries and where the rarer ones are to be found. It is very much fuller than any existing list of Lancashire directories and should therefore be of great value to historians.

It is hoped to follow this list of Directories with the publication of a list of Local Acts relating to Lancashire. This in turn, it is hoped, will be followed by the publication of other sections of the Bibliography on a subject basis. In this way the largest and fullest county bibliography that has so far been attempted should become available to libraries and to scholars.

T. S. WILLAN
Chairman of the Joint Committee

PREFACE

From a cursory examination of the material which my predecessor, Dr. Tupling, had prepared as the basis for this list, it was clear that he intended to draw upon the detailed information included by Jane E. Norton in her *Guide to the national and provincial directories of England and Wales, excluding London, published before 1856* (Royal Historical Society, 1950). I, too, have been greatly influenced by her work and take this early opportunity of expressing my appreciation of her skill, patience and scholarship.

With the present list, covering as it does an extended period during which the publication of directories became more prolific, it was impossible to follow the same lines of treatment. Time and expense were the main enemies. Where applicable, however, the Norton reference numbers have been included, thus reducing the size of the work and consequently its cost. With the generous co-operation of librarians in the North-West, it has been possible to increase considerably the number of locations of copies of directories which she included.

The present work comprises, primarily, town and county directories, alphabetical and classified telephone directories and a small selection of trades, professional and official directories of peculiar significance to Lancashire. Electoral rolls, voters' lists, poll books and similar sources of directory-type information have not been included. Manuals published by municipal authorities, often the source of much useful information, will appear in a later part.

Librarians in the North-West will immediately recognize the system of recording the locations of copies of an item. The numbers are, of course, those used by the North Western Regional Library Bureau, a list of which immediately precedes the main chronological list together with other abbreviations. Should there be any variations in a library's holdings, either by reasons of addition or by withdrawal, it would be appreciated if librarians would kindly notify the Editor.

During my editorship, I have been greatly assisted by my staff, Mrs. P. M. Turner, B.A., and Mrs. Olga Thomson, and to them I am deeply indebted for their loyal and enthusiastic support ; without their aid, it would have been impossible to produce this list. My thanks are also due to members of the staffs of the Reference and Local History Libraries, The Manchester Public Libraries, who from time to time have been seconded to the Bibliography Office ; to Mr. D. I. Colley, M.A., F.L.A., and to my former colleagues, I am extremely grateful for their interest and help.

SIDNEY HORROCKS
Editor

CONTENTS

KEY TO LOCATION NUMBERS AND ABBREVIATIONS

* Holdings of ten or more copies are indicated by the use of an asterisk.

C Chetham's Library

HS Historic Society of Lancashire and Cheshire

RO Lancashire County Record Office

D/d Directory/directories

1	Manchester	31	Middleton
1AS	Lancashire and Cheshire Antiquarian Society	32	Nelson
		33	Rawtenstall
3	Lancashire County	34	Widnes
5	Barrow-in-Furness	35	Ashton-in-Makerfield
6	Blackburn	36	Atherton
7	Bolton	37	Chadderton
8	Bootle	38	Clayton-le-Moors
9	Burnley	39	Crompton
10	Bury	41	Denton
11	Oldham	42	Failsworth
12	Preston	43	Farnworth
13	Rochdale	44	Fleetwood
14	St. Helens	45	Crosby
15	Salford	47	Milnrow
16	Southport	48	Newton-le-Willows
17	Warrington	49†	Oswaldtwistle
18	Wigan	50	Radcliffe
19	Accrington	51	Royton
20	Ashton-under-Lyne	52	Stretford
21	Bacup	53	Swinton and Pendlebury
22	Chorley	54†	Tyldesley-with-Shakerley
23	Colne	56	Westhoughton
24	Darwen	59	Stockport
25	Eccles	72	Todmorden
26	Haslingden	75†	Littleborough
27	Heywood	79	Liverpool University
28	Lancaster	85	Manchester University
29	Leigh	88	Clitheroe
30	Lytham St. Annes	92	Blackpool

†These authorities are now included for library purposes with Lancashire County Library. The numbers are now allocated to other libraries.

CHRONOLOGICAL LIST

1684–1957

1684

1/1   DOCTON, K. H., (comp.). A d. of Lancaster. Lancaster,
1954.   1,12,28,C,RO
       Later reprinted in HS., 109, pp. 125–42.   *

1766

1/2   GORE, JOHN. The Liverpool d. . . . containing an alphabetical
list of the merchants, tradesmen, and principal inhabitants
of the town of Liverpool, with their respective addresses.
Liv., 1766. (Reprint).   1,14,17,79

1/3   SHAW, G. T., & SHAW, ISABELLA, (comp.).   Liverpool's
first d.: a reprint of the names and addresses from
Gore's D. for 1766; to which is added a street d. for the
same year compiled by G. T. Shaw and Isabella Shaw; also
a history of the Liverpool d. from 1766 to 1907; by
G. T. Shaw. Liv., 1907.   *

1767

1/4   SHAW, G. T., & SHAW, ISABELLA, (comp.).   Liverpool's
second d.: a reprint of the names and addresses from
Gore's D. for 1767; to which are added a street d., and
lists of professional men and tradesmen. Liv., 1928.
       1,8,79,RO

1769

1/5   SHAW, G. T., & SHAW, ISABELLA, (comp.).   Liverpool's
third d.: a reprint of the names and addresses from
Gore's D. for 1769; to which are added a street d., and
lists of professional men and tradesmen. Liv., 1930.
       1,8,16,79,RO

1772

1/6   RAFFALD, ELIZABETH. The Manchester d.: containing an
alphabetical list of the merchants, tradesmen, and principal
inhabitants in the town of Manchester. 1772. (Norton,
487).   1

1/7   — The Manchester d. Manch., 1889.   *
       A reprint published for R. H. Sutton.

1773

1/8   RAFFALD, ELIZABETH. The Manchester d. Manch., 1773.
        (Norton, 488).   1,15,53,C,RO

1/9   — The Manchester d. Manch., 1889.   *
        Reprinted for Albert Sutton, with a prefatory memoir.

1/10   SHAW, G. T., & SHAW, ISABELLA, (comp.).   Liverpool's
        fourth d.: a reprint of the names and addresses from
        Gore's D. for 1773; to which are added a street d., and
        lists of professional men and tradesmen. Liv., 1931.   1,8,79,RO

1774

1/11   GORE, JOHN. The Liverpool d. Liv., [1774]. (Norton, 440).   1,RO

1/12   SHAW, G. T., & SHAW, ISABELLA, (comp.).   Liverpool's
        fifth d.: a reprint of the names and addresses from
        Gore's D. for 1774; to which are added a street d., and
        lists of professional men and tradesmen. Liv., 1932.   1,8,79,RO

1777

1/13   GORE, JOHN. Liverpool d. Liv., [1777]. (Norton, 441).   RO

1781

1/14   BAILEY, WILLIAM. Northern d.: containing . . . every princi-
        pal town from the River Trent to Berwick-upon-Tweed.
        Warrington, 1781. (Norton, 1).   13,RO

1/15   RAFFALD, ELIZABETH.   The Manchester and Salford d.
        [Manch.], 1781. (Norton, 489).   1,7,15,59,C

1787

1/16   TUNNICLIFF, WILLIAM.   A topographical survey of the
        counties of Stafford, Chester and Lancaster. Nantwich,
        1787. (Norton, 6).   *
        Includes d. of the principal merchants, etc., in Stockport, Lan-
        caster, Kirkham, Blackburn, Bolton, Burnley, Bury, Rochdale,
        Bacup, Rossendale, Haslingden, Prescot, Preston, Leigh, Warrington,
        Ormskirk, Wigan, Ulverston, Manchester, Liverpool.

1788

1/17   [HOLME, EDMOND]. A d. for the towns of Manchester and
        Salford. Manch., [1788]. (Norton, 490).   1,15,17,C,RO

1/18   — Lewis's D. for the towns of Manchester and Salford.
        Manch., 1888.   1,11,14,16,25,29,31,C,RO

1789

1/19   COWDROY, WILLIAM. The d. and guide for Chester . . . [and]
        market towns throughout the county. Chester, 1789.
        (Norton, 139).   59
        Stockport section only. (Photocopy).

1/20   TUNNICLIFF, WILLIAM.   A topographical survey of the counties of Somerset . . . Chester, and Lancaster. Bath, 1789. (Norton, 7).   **1**

Includes d. of merchants and manufacturers in Stockport, Lancaster, Kirkham, Blackburn, Bolton, Burnley, Bury, Rochdale, Bacup, Rossendale, Haslingden, Prescot, Preston, Leigh, Warrington, Ormskirk, Wigan, Ulverston, Manchester, Liverpool; also seats of gentry in Lancashire.

1790

1/21   GORE, JOHN. Lewis's Liverpool d.: an alphabetical list of the merchants, tradesmen and principal inhabitants. 1890.   **1,17,RO**

The "Sketch of Liverpool" from Gore's 1796 d. added.

1790–8

1/22   THE UNIVERSAL British d. of trade and commerce: inhabitants of London . . . the cities, towns and principal villages in England and Wales. 1790–8. 4v. (Norton, 8, 13, 15, 18).   1(v.1–3),8(v.3),13(v.4),17(v.4),RO(v.4)

v.1, London; v.2–4, The Provinces.
v.2 includes Bolton, Burnley, Bury, Cartmel, Chorley, Clitheroe. 1793.
v.3 includes Garstang, Hawkshead, Lancaster, Leigh, Liverpool, Manchester and Salford. 1794.
v.4 includes Rochdale, Warrington, Newton-le-Willows and Prescot. 1798.

1794

1/23   SCHOLES, JOHN. Manchester and Salford d. Manch., 1794. (Norton, 491).   **1,15,29,85,C**

1796

1/24   GORE, JOHN. Liverpool d.: or, alphabetical list of the merchants. Liv., 1796. (Norton, 447).   **RO**

1797

1/25   SCHOLES, JOHN. Manchester and Salford d. 2nd ed. Manch., 1797. (Norton, 492).   **1,15,18,59,85,C**

1800

1/26   BANCKS, GERARD. Manchester and Salford d. Manch., 1800. (Norton, 493).   **1,15,29,85,C**

1/27   GORE, JOHN. Liverpool d. Liv., 1800. (Norton, 448).   **79,RO**

1802

1/28   BANCKS, GERARD. Manchester and Salford d. Manch., 1802. (Norton, 494).   **1,15,29,C**

1803

1/29   GORE, JOHN, & SON. Liverpool d. Liv., 1803. (Norton, 450).   **1,RO**

1804

1/30   DEAN, R. & W., & CO. Manchester and Salford d. Manch., 1804. (Norton, 495).   1,13,15,C

1805

1/31   GORE, JOHNSON. D. of Liverpool. Liv., 1805. (Norton, 453).   79

1805–06–07

1/32   HOLDEN, WILLIAM. Triennial d. 4th ed. 1805. 2v. (Norton, 21).   1,C
> v.2 contains commercial d. of Blackburn, Bolton, Lancaster, Liverpool, Manchester, Preston, Rochdale, Stockport, Warrington, Wigan.

1807

1/33   GORE, JOHNSON. The Liverpool d. Liv., 1807. (Norton, 454).   1,C

1808

1/34   DEAN, R. & W., & CO. Manchester and Salford d. for 1808 and 1809. Manch., 1808. (Norton, 496).   1,15,C

1809–10–11

1/35   HOLDEN, WILLIAM. Triennial d. 5th ed. 1809. 2v. (Norton, 23).   1,17(Warr.only),28
> v.2 contains commercial d. of Blackburn, Bolton, Bury, Lancaster, Liverpool, Manchester, Preston, Rochdale, Stockport, Warrington, Wigan.

1810

1/36   GORE, JOHNSON. D. of Liverpool and its environs. Liv., 1810. (Norton, 445).   1,8

1811

1/37   DEAN, R. & W., & CO. Manchester and Salford d. Manch., 1811. (Norton, 497).   1,15

1/38   PIGOT, JAMES. Manchester and Salford d. Manch., [1810]. (Norton, 498).   1,29,C
> Contains rather more names than Dean, 1811.

1813

1/39   GORE, JOHNSON. D. of Liverpool and its environs. Liv., 1813. (Norton, 457).   17

1/40   PIGOT, JAMES. Manchester and Salford d. Manch., 1813. (Norton, 499).   1,15,27,29,59,C,RO

1814–15

1/41   WARDLE, M., & BENTHAM. The commercial d. Manch., 1814. (Norton, 29).   1,9,13,14,20,22,C,RO
> Includes d. of Ashton-under-Lyne, Blackburn, Bolton, Burnley, Bury, Chorley, Colne, Lancaster, Liverpool, Manchester, Oldham, Prescot, Preston, Rochdale, Stockport, Warrington, Wigan.

1/42   PIGOT, JAMES, & DEAN, R. & W. Manchester and Salford d.
Manch., 1815. (Norton, 500).   1,13,C,RO

1816–17

1/43   HOLDEN, WILLIAM. Annual d. Class first . . . merchants,
shipowners, bankers [and] class second . . . agents, brokers,
brewers . . . in London and 480 . . . towns. 1816. (Norton,
26).   1,13,20,72,C,RO
>   Includes d. for Bacup, Blackburn, Bolton, Burnley, Bury, Cartmel
>   (class one only), Chorley, Chowbent (class second only), Colne,
>   Garstang, Haslingden (class one only), Kirkham and Freckleton
>   (class second only), Lancaster, Leigh, Liverpool, Manchester, Old-
>   ham, Ormskirk, Poulton, Prescot, Preston, Rochdale, Stockport,
>   Warrington, Wigan.

1/44   WARDLE, M., & PRATT. The commercial d. Manch., 1816.
(Norton, 30).   1,7,59,C
>   Includes d. of Ashton-under-Lyne, Blackburn, Bolton, Burnley,
>   Bury, Chorley, Colne, Lancaster, Liverpool, Manchester, Oldham,
>   Prescot, Preston, Rochdale, Stockport, Warrington, Wigan.

1817

1/45   BUTTERWORTH, JAMES. An historical and descriptive account
of . . . Oldham . . . with a d. Oldham, 1817. (Norton, 530).   *

1/46   PIGOT, JAMES, & DEAN, R. & W. Manchester and Salford d.
Manch., 1817. (Norton, 501).   1,17,C

1818

1/47   GORE, JOHNSON. D. of Liverpool and its environs. Liv.,
1818. (Norton, 460).   79

1/48   ROGERSON, T. Lancashire general d. Manch., [1818].
(Norton, 419).
           1,7(pt.2),9(pt.2),10(pt.2),13(pt.2),19,22,C,RO(pts.1,2)
>   Pt. 1 includes Blackburn, Accrington, Church, Clitheroe, Darwen
>   and Whalley.
>   Pt. 2 includes Bolton [and suburbs] and Leigh.
>   Pt. 3 includes Preston with Chorley and Walton.

1818–19–20

1/49   LEIGH, J. Lancashire general d. Manch., 1818. (Norton,
421).   1,11,C
>   Pt. 2 includes Ashton-under-Lyne, Burnley, Bury, Colne, Middle-
>   ton, Oldham, Rochdale [and surrounding villages].

1/50   PIGOT, JAMES, & DEAN, R. & W. The commercial d. Manch.,
1818. (Norton, 31).   1,9,12,13,17(Warr.only),22,28,C
>   Includes directories of Ashton-under-Lyne, Blackburn, Bolton,
>   Burnley, Bury, Chorley, Colne, Lancaster, Liverpool, Manchester,
>   Oldham, Prescot, Preston, Rochdale, St. Helens, Stockport, War-
>   rington, Wigan.

1819–20

/51   PIGOT, JAMES, & DEAN, R. & W. The commercial d. Manch.,
1819. (Norton, 32).   14

1/52   PIGOT, JAMES, & DEAN, R. & W. Manchester and Salford d.
       Manch., 1819. (Norton, 502).   1,9,C

1820

1/53   BUTTERWORTH, JAMES. A description and d. of . . . Rochdale.
       Manch., 1820. (Norton, 533).   11,13

1821

1/54   GORE, JOHNSON. Liverpool d. with its environs. Liv., 1821.
       (Norton, 461).   1,RO

1/55   WHITTLE, PETER, (Tulket, Marmaduke, pseud.). A topo-
       graphical, statistical, and historical account of the borough
       of Preston: . . . including . . . a d. Preston, 1821. (Norton,
       531).   1,6,13,RO

1821–2

1/56   PIGOT, JAMES, & DEAN, R. & W. New d. of Manchester and
       Salford, . . . [with places] twelve miles round Manchester.
       Manch., 1821. (Norton, 503).   1,10,13,25,59,C,RO

1822–3

1/57   PIGOT, JAMES, & CO. London and provincial new commercial
       d.   Manch., [1822]. (Norton, 35).   1,17(Warr.only),28,C
       Includes thirty-one towns in Lancashire; also Stockport.

1823

1/58   GORE, JOHNSON. Liverpool d. with its environs. Liv., 1823.
       (Norton, 462).   1,C,RO

1824–5

1/59   BAINES, EDWARD, the elder. History, d. and gazetteer of
       the County Palatine of Lancaster; the d. department by
       W. Parson. Liv., 1824–5. (Norton, 422).
                           1,7(Bolton only),18(Wigan only),C,RO

1/60   PIGOT, JAMES, & DEAN, R. & W. D. for Manchester, Salford,
       . . . [with places] within twenty-four miles. Manch., 1824.
       (Norton, 504).   7(Bolton only),*

1825

1/61   GORE, JOHNSON. Liverpool d. with its environs. Liv., 1825.
       (Norton, 463).   1

1826

1/62   GLAZEBROOK, T. K. A guide to Southport, North Meols . . .
       with an account of the places in its immediate neighbour-
       hood. 2nd ed. 1826. (Norton, 534).   1,3,12,16,17,48,85,RO

1827

1/63   GORE, JOHNSON, & SON. D. of Liverpool and its environs.
       Liv., 1827. (Norton, 464).   RO

1/64   PICKEN, ANDREW, & SON. Annual d. of Liverpool and its environs. Liv., [1827]. (Norton, 481).   1

1828

1/65   PIGOT, JAMES, & CO. New commercial d. for Cheshire, Derbyshire and Lancashire. Manch., 1828. (Norton, 48).   1,5

1/66   WARDLE, M., & WILKINSON, T. The Manchester and Salford director and memorandum book. Manch., 1828. (Norton, 505).   1,15,C

1828–9

1/67   PIGOT, JAMES, & CO. National commercial d. [for] Cheshire, Cumberland . . . Lancashire. Manch., [1828]. (Norton, 47).   1,8,10,12,17(Warr.only),25(Eccles only),C

1829

1/68   GORE, JOHNSON, & SON. D. of Liverpool and its environs. Liv., 1829. (Norton, 466).   1,RO

1/69   PARSON, WILLIAM, & WHITE, WILLIAM. History, d. and gazetteer of . . . Cumberland and Westmorland, with . . . Furness and Cartmel. Leeds, 1829. (Norton, 158).   3,5,59,C

1/70   PIGOT, JAMES, & SON. General d. of Manchester, Salford. Manch., 1829. (Norton, 507).   1,10,11,18,C

1/71   WARDLE, M. The Bolton director. [1829]. (Norton, 432).   1,7,C

1/72   — & WILKINSON, T. The Manchester and Salford director. Manch., 1829. (Norton, 506).   1,15,29,C

1830

1/73   SYERS, ROBERT. The history of Everton, including familiar dissertations on the people, and descriptive delineations of the several and separate properties of the township. Liv., 1830. (Norton, 482).   1,8,15,19,RO

1/74   PIGOT, JAMES, & SON. General d. of Manchester. Manch., [1830]. (Norton, 508).   1,C

1/75   WHITTLE, P., & WHITTLE, H. A history [with a d.] of Lytham. [Preston, 1830].   1,12,16,C

1830–1

1/76   PIGOT, JAMES, & CO. New commercial d. for the counties of Cheshire, Derbyshire and Lancashire. Manch., 1830–1. (Norton, 50).   29,C

1831

1/77   WHITTLE, PETER. Marina, or an historical account of Southport, Lytham and Blackpool. Preston, 1831. (Norton, 535).   16,RO

1/78   ALSOP, WILLIAM. A concise history of Southport, a fashion-
        able watering place situate in North Meols . . . together
        with a tide table and d. Southport, [1832]. (Norton, 536).   1,RO

1/79   GORE, JOHNSON, & SON. D. and view of Liverpool and its
        environs. Liv., 1832. (Norton, 468).   1,29

1/80   PIGOT, JAMES, & SON. General and classified d. of Manchester
        . . . also [places] within twelve miles. Manch., 1832.
        (Norton, 509).   1,11,13,20,27,C

1833

1/81   PIGOT, JAMES, & SON. General and classified d. of Manchester
        . . . also [places] within twelve miles . . . with an addenda
        for 1833. Manch., 1833. (Norton, 510).   C,RO

1834

1/82   MAWDSLEY, J. & J. Gore's D. and view of Liverpool and its
        environs. Liv., 1834. (Norton, 469).   1,8,RO

1/84   PIGOT, JAMES, & CO. National commercial d. [for] the
        counties of Chester, Cumberland, Durham, Lancaster.
        Manch., 1834. (Norton, 61).
                  1,7(Bolton only),9,14,17,31,59(Stockport only),RO

1835

1/85   MAWDSLEY, J. & J. Gore's D. of Liverpool and its environs.
        Liv., 1835. (Norton, 470).   1,79,RO

1/86   ROBINSON, C. An historical and descriptive account of . . .
        Chorley . . . to which is added a d. of Chorley. Chorley,
        1835. (Norton, 435).   22

1836

1/87   PIGOT, JAMES, & SON. General and classified d. of Man-
        chester and Salford . . . also [places] within twelve miles of
        Manchester. Manch., 1836. (Norton, 512).   1,C

1837

1/88   MAWDSLEY, J. & J. Gore's D. of Liverpool and its environs.
        Liv., 1837. (Norton, 471).   1

1/89   PIGOT, JAMES, & CO. D. of Scotland and the Isle of Man
        [with trade d. for Manchester and Liverpool]. 1837.
        (Norton, 64).   1

1838

1/90   PIGOT, JAMES, & SON. General, classified and street d. of
        Manchester and Salford . . . [with places] within twelve
        miles . . . and some others . . . more distant. Manch., 1838.
        (Norton, 513).   18(Wigan only),*

1839

1/91   MAWDSLEY, J. & J. Gore's D. of Liverpool and its environs.
Liv., 1839. (Norton, 472).   1,8,79

1840

1/92   PIGOT, JAMES, & SLATER, ISAAC.   General, classified and
street d. of Manchester. Manch., 1840. (Norton, 514).
                                          1,85,C,RO

1841

1/93   MAWDSLEY, JAMES. Gore's D. of Liverpool and its environs.
Liv., 1841. (Norton, 473).   1,8,RO

1/94   PIGOT, JAMES, & CO. Royal national and commercial d. and
topography of the counties of York . . . [with] classified d.
of Manchester and Salford and alphabetical ones of . . .
towns and villages. Manch., 1841. (Norton, 70).   1

1/95   — & SLATER, ISAAC. Classified, commercial d. of Manchester and Salford . . . [with places] within twelve miles
. . . and some others. Manch., 1841. (Norton, 516).
            1,7,17,18,25(Eccles only),59,C,RO

1/96   — — General, classified and street d. of Manchester . . .
[with places] within twelve miles and some others.
Manch., 1841. (Norton, 515).   1,10

1/97   [WARRINGTON RADICAL PARTY]. The Black list. 2nd ed.
Warrington, printed by Thomas Hurst, [1841].   17
        A list of Conservative tradesmen in Warrington, published by the
        Radicals.

1/98   WHITTLE, P. & H. Commercial d. of Preston and its environs.
Preston, 1841.   12,RO

1843

1/99   MAWDSLEY, JAMES. Gore's D. of Liverpool and its environs.
Liv., 1843. (Norton, 474).   1,79

1/100   PIGOT, JAMES, & SLATER, ISAAC. General and classified d.
and street register of Liverpool, its suburbs and vicinity.
Manch., 1843. (Norton, 484).   1,17,79,C

1/101   — — General and classified d. and street registers of Manchester and Liverpool, their suburbs and vicinities . . .
[and] the Isle of Man. Manch., 1843. (Norton, 518).   13,C

1/102   — — General and classified d. and street register of Manchester and Salford. Manch., 1843. (Norton, 517).   1,13,85,C

1/103   SLATER, ISAAC. A d. of Manchester and Salford and the
townships contiguous. Manch., 1843. (Norton, 519).
                                  1,11,20,28,C

1/104   — A d. of the towns and principal villages . . . round Manchester. Manch., 1843. (Norton, 520).   25(Eccles only),C

1/105   SLATER, ISAAC. D. of Liverpool and its environs, and other towns more distant. Manch., 1844. (Norton, 484, re-issue).   1,17,28

1/106   — A d. of towns in the environs of Liverpool, with others more distant in Cheshire and Lancashire and exclusive of those in the manufacturing district. Manch., 1844.   1,C

1/107   — A d. of the towns and principal villages throughout the extensive manufacturing district round Manchester. Manch., 1844. (Norton, 77).   18(Wigan only),20,27,C

1845

1/108   MAWDSLEY, JAMES. Gore's D. of Liverpool and its environs. Liv., 1845. (Norton, 475).   1,8,79,RO

1/109   SLATER, ISAAC. General and classified d. and street register of Manchester and Salford and their vicinities. Manch., 1845. (Norton, 521).   1,15,85,C

1/110   WILLIAMS, J. Commercial d. of Preston, Wigan, Bolton, Blackburn, Accrington, Darwen, Bury, Oldham, Rochdale, Burnley, . . .; also classified lists of the merchants and manufacturers of Manchester. 1845.   26

1/111   — Commercial d. of Stockport, Preston, Wigan . . . Manch., 1845. (Norton, 140).   59,C

1/112   — D. of Bolton, Rochdale, Bury, Oldham, Burnley, Bacup. Manch., 1845.   1,7(Bolton only),RO

1/113   — D. of Rochdale, Bacup, Heywood and numerous villages in the vicinity; also classified lists of the merchants and manufacturers of Manchester and Leeds. Rochdale, 1845.   1,13

1846

1/114   SLATER, ISAAC. D. of Ireland . . . with Birmingham . . . Liverpool, Manchester. Manch., 1846. (Norton, 81).   C

1/115   WILLIAMS, J. Commercial d. of . . . Chester . . . Stockport. 1846. (Norton, 141).   1
        Includes also Warrington, Wigan, Gorton, Fairfield, Openshaw and Droylsden.

1847

1/116   LOVE & BARTON. Manchester Exchange d. Manch., 1847. 1,11,C

1/117   MAWDSLEY, JAMES. Gore's D. of Liverpool and its environs. Liv., 1847. (Norton, 476).   1

1848

1/118   LOVE & BARTON. Manchester Exchange d. Manch., 1848. 1,11,C

1/119   ROBINSON, FRANK. A descriptive history of the popular watering-place of Southport in the parish of North Meols. 1848. (Norton, 538).   1,16,19,29

1/120   SLATER, ISAAC. General and classified d. and street register of Manchester and Salford. Manch., 1848. (Norton, 523). 1,15,C

1/121   — Royal national commercial d. and topography of the counties of . . . Lancaster. Manch., 1848. (Norton, 83).
1,18(Wigan only),33

1849

1/122   MANNEX, P., & CO. History, topography, and d. of Westmorland and Lonsdale north of the sands in Lancashire. 1849. (Norton, 756).   12

1/123   MAWDSLEY, JAMES. Gore's D. of Liverpool and its environs. Liv., 1849. (Norton, 477).   1

1/124   POORE, J. A guide to Southport and the surrounding neighbourhood and parish. Liv., 1849. (Norton, 539).   16,RO

1850

1/125   BAGSHAW, SAMUEL. History, gazetteer and d. of the county . . . of Chester. Sheffield, 1850. (Norton, 142).   1,59

1/126   HEAP, JOHN. The Bury d. Bury, 1850. (Norton, 534).   1,10,27

1/127   SLATER, ISAAC. General and classified d. and street register of Manchester and Salford. Manch., 1850. (Norton, 524). 1,85,C

1851

1/128   MANNEX, P., & CO. The history, topography, and d. of the borough of Preston and seven miles round; with the town and parish of Chorley. Beverley, 1851. (Norton, 532).   1,9,12,22,28,RO

1/129   — History, topography and d. of Westmorland and of the Hundreds of Lonsdale and Amounderness in Lancashire. Beverley, 1851. (Norton, 757).   1,3,28

1/130   MAWDSLEY, JAMES, & SON. Gore's D. of Liverpool and its environs. Liv., 1851. (Norton, 478).   1,8,79

1/131   OAKEY, HENRY. Commercial d. of Preston. Preston, 1851.   RO

1/132   SLATER, ISAAC. Alphabetical and classified d. of Manchester and Salford and their vicinities . . ., classified d. of the towns and villages within . . . twelve miles. Manch., 1851. (Norton, 525).   1,13,15,20,C

1/133   — Classified commercial d. of the towns and villages in the extensive manufacturing district round Manchester. Manch., 1851.   C

1/134   — Royal national classified commercial d. and topography of the county of Lancashire and the manufacturing district. Manch., 1851. (Norton, 92).   1,3,17(Warr. only),85,RO

1/135   — Royal national classified commercial d. and topography of the county of Lancashire (excepting Manchester). Manch., 1851. (Norton, 93).   1,10,12,85

1/136   SLATER, ISAAC. Commercial d. of the Isle of Man [with] Manchester, Birmingham . . . Liverpool. Manch., 1852. (Norton, 95).   C

1/137   — General and classified d. and street register of Manchester and Salford with their vicinities . . . with a classified d. . . . of the whole of Lancashire. Manch., 1852. (Norton, 94).   1,C

1/138   WHELLAN, WM., & Co. A new alphabetical and classified d. of Manchester and Salford and [vicinity]. Manch., 1852. (Norton, 427).   1,13,15,29,C

1/139   WHITTLE, PETER. Blackburn as it is : a topographical, statistical and historical account of the borough of Blackburn, [with] a d. Preston, 1852. (Norton, 431).   *

1/140   MAWDSLEY, JAMES, & SON. Gore's D. of Liverpool and its environs. Liv., 1853. (Norton, 479).   1,79,RO

1/141   OAKEY, HENRY. Commercial and trade d. of Preston. Preston, 1853.   12,RO

1/142   WHELLAN, WM., & Co. A new alphabetical and classified d. of Manchester and Salford, Bolton, Bury, Wigan, Ashton-under-Lyne, Stalybridge, etc. Manch., 1853. (Norton, 428).   1,10,14(St. Helens only),15,C

1/143   — A new alphabetical and classified d. of the boroughs of Bolton, Bury, and Wigan, the parishes of Dean and Leigh. Manch., 1853.   18

1/144   MANNEX, P., & Co. History, topography and d. of mid-Lancashire, with an essay on geology. Preston, 1854. (Norton, 430).   *

1/145   COLLINSON & Co. The Manchester mercantile and manufacturing annual d. Manch., 1855. (Norton, 529).   1,C

1/146   SLATER, ISAAC. Royal national commercial d. of the northern counties. Manch., 1854–5. 2v. (Norton, 99).   1,17,34(Widnes only),59
      v.2. Cheshire, Cumberland, Lancashire, Westmorland . . . the towns of Liverpool and Manchester. Manch., 1855.

1/147   MANNEX, P., & Co. History, topography and d. of mid-Lancashire with an essay on geology. Preston, 1855.   14,22,34(Widnes only)

1/148   MAWDSLEY, JAMES, & SON. Gore's D. for Liverpool and its environs. Liv., 1855. (Norton, 480).   1,8,79,C

1/149 SLATER, ISAAC. General and classified d. and street register of Manchester and Salford [and vicinity]. Manch., 1855. (Norton, 528).   1,C

1856

1/150 SLATER, ISAAC. Commercial d. and topography of Lancashire. Manch., 1856.   1

1857

1/151 GILLBANKS, B. H., & Co. D. and gazetteer of the watering places of Lancashire: Southport, Blackpool, Fleetwood, Lytham and Morecambe Bay. 1857.   16

1/152 KELLY & Co. D. of Cheshire. 1857.   1,59

1/153 MAWDSLEY, JAMES, & SON. Gore's D. for Liverpool and its environs. Liv., 1857.   1,79

1/154 SLATER, ISAAC. Royal national commercial d. of . . . Manchester, Birmingham. Manch., 1857.   1,C

1858

1/155 KELLY & Co. Post Office d. of Lancashire. 1858.
1,18(Wigan only),27

1/156 — Post Office d. of Liverpool and Manchester. 1858.   1

1/157 — Post Office d. of Manchester. 1858.   1

1/157A PORTER, WILLIAM. Guide to Blackpool: with notices of Fleetwood, Lytham, etc., together with a d. of Blackpool, and a map of the Fylde district. Blackpool, 1858.   1,13

1/158 SLATER, ISAAC. General and classified d. and street register of Manchester and Salford. Manch., 1858.   1,C

1/159 — Royal national commercial d. of Manchester and Liverpool, and the principal manufacturing towns in Lancashire, etc. Manch., 1858.   22,59,C

1/160 TURNER, JOHN. Rochdale d. and almanack. Rochdale, 1858.   13

1859

1/161 MAWDSLEY, JAMES, & SON. Gore's D. for Liverpool and its environs. Liv., 1859.   1,8,45

1/162 PORTER, WILLIAM. Annual guide and visitor's companion to Blackpool, Fleetwood, Lytham, etc., together with a d. of Blackpool, and a map of the Fylde district. [3rd ed.]. Blackpool, 1859.   3

1860

1/163 WHITE, FRANCIS, & Co. History, gazetteer and d. of Cheshire. Sheffield, 1860.   1,59,C

1861

1/164   DRAKE, E. S.   Commercial d. of Bolton, Bury, Wigan, Chorley, Darwen, Leigh, Radcliffe, Ramsbottom [and adjoining townships]. Sheffield, 1861.   7,C

1/165   SLATER, ISAAC. General and classified d. and street register of Manchester and Salford with their vicinities . . . Manch., 1861.   C

1/166   — Royal national commercial d. of Manchester and Liverpool, and the principal manufacturing towns in Lancashire. Manch., 1861.   1,13,17(Warr. only),52,C

1862

1/167   MAWDSLEY, J., & SON. Gore's D. for Liverpool and its environs. Liv., 1862.   45

1863

1/168   SLATER, ISAAC. General and classified d. and street register of Manchester and Salford, with their vicinities. Manch., 1863.   1,C

1/169   — Royal national commercial d. of Birmingham, Glasgow, Liverpool and Manchester. Manch., 1863.   1

1864

1/170   KELLY & CO. D. of Cheshire. 1864.   1

1/171   — The Post Office d. of Lancaster and its vicinity. 1864.   28

1/172   — The Post Office d. of Lancashire, Liverpool and Manchester. 1864.   1,17,28

1/173   MAWDSLEY, J., & SON. Gore's D. for Liverpool and its environs. Liv., 1864.   1

1/174   MORRIS & CO. Commercial d. and gazetteer of Cheshire. 1864.   1,59

1/175   ROBERTSON, J., & CO. Trade d. of Manchester and Salford. Manch., 1864.   15

1864–5

1/176   ROBERTSON, J., & CO. D. of Blackburn, Accrington, Church and district. Manch., 1864.   19

1865

1/177   KELLY & CO. D. of Cheshire. 1865.   1

1/178   MANNEX, P., & CO. Preston and district: being the first volume of the d. and topography of north Lancashire. Preston, 1865.   12

1/179   MAWDSLEY, J., & SON. Gore's D. for Liverpool and its environs. Liv., 1865.   1

1/180   SLATER, ISAAC. General and classified d. and street register of Manchester and Salford with their vicinities. Manch., 1865.   1,C

1/181   — Royal national commercial d. of Lancashire. Manch., 1865.   1,33,59

1866

1/182   MANNEX, P., & CO. D. and topography of Southport and north Lancashire district ; with an essay on geology. Preston, 1866.   3,16,22,24,28,92

1/182A   PORTER, WILLIAM. Guide to Blackpool, Fleetwood, Lytham, etc. : with a d. of Blackpool. Blackpool and Fleetwood, 1866.   1,16,19,29,92

1867

1/183   MAWDSLEY, J., & SON. Gore's D. for Liverpool and its environs. Liv., 1867.   1,8

1868

1/184   GREEN, B. L., (comp.). The official d. of Southport and Birkdale. 1868.   16

1/185   MANNEX, P., & CO. D. of Blackburn and east Lancashire. Preston, 1868.   19

1/186   — D. of north and east Lancashire, . . . with historical sketches of Furness and Whalley Abbeys. Preston, 1868.   9,12

1/187   MAWDSLEY, J., & SON. Gore's D. for Liverpool and its environs. Liv., 1868.   1

1868–9

1/188   MORRIS, J. S. C. The business d. of Manchester. 1868.   1,C

1869

1/189   GILLETT, G. A. Commercial and general d. of Preston, including the townships of Ashton, Fulwood, Penwortham and Walton-le-Dale. Preston, 1869.   12

1/190   SLATER, ISAAC. General and classified d. and street register of Manchester and Salford with their vicinities. Manch., 1869.   1,C

1/191   — Royal national commercial d. of Cheshire and Lancashire. Manch., 1869.   1,17

1/192   — Royal national commercial d. of Lancashire. Manch., 1869.   1

1/193   WORRALL, JOHN. The Wigan d. Blackburn, 1869.   1,18,29

1870

1/194   GREEN, A., & CO. D. for Liverpool and Birkenhead. 1870.   1

1/195 MAWDSLEY, J., & SON. Gore's D. for Liverpool and its environs. Liv., 1870.   1

1870–1

1/196 WORRALL, JOHN. Blackburn and Darwen d. Blackburn, [1870].   6

1/197 — The Bolton and district d. . . . , comprising all the townships in the Bolton Union. Bolton, [1870].   7

1871

1/198 MANNEX, P., & Co. D. and historical sketches, . . . of St. Helens and district. Preston, 1871.   14,17

1/199 NORTH LONSDALE PRINTING Co. Commercial d. of the borough of Barrow-in-Furness. Barrow, [1871?].   5

1/200 PORTER, WILLIAM. Guide to Blackpool, Fleetwood, Lytham, etc., with a d. of Blackpool. 8th ed. Blackpool, [1871].   3,12

1/201 WORRALL, JOHN. D. of Bury and Bolton with the parishes and townships of Heywood, Radcliffe, Ramsbottom, Farnworth, and neighbourhoods. Oldham, 1871.   10,50

1/202 — D. of Oldham, Ashton-under-Lyne, Stalybridge, Dukinfield, Guide Bridge, Saddleworth and Middleton. Oldham, 1871.   11,29

1/203 — D. of Warrington, St. Helens, Prescot, Leigh, Newton-le-Willows, Widnes, . . . and adjoining townships. Oldham, 1871.   14,17,C

1871–2

1/204 SLATER, ISAAC. General and classified d. and street register of Manchester and Salford with their vicinities. Manch., 1871–2.   1,C

1/205 — Royal national commercial d. of Lancashire. Manch., 1871.   1,C

1872

1/206 MAWDSLEY, J., & SON. Gore's D. for Liverpool and its environs. Liv., 1872.   1

1/207 WORRALL, JOHN. D. of Chorley. Oldham, 1872.   RO

1/208 — D. of Stockport, Heaton Norris, and adjoining townships. Oldham, 1872.   59

1/209 — Wigan and district d., with Chorley, Ormskirk and adjoining townships. 2nd ed. Oldham, 1872.   3,18,22,RO

1873

1/210 KELLY & Co. The Post Office d. of Lancashire, Liverpool and Manchester. 1873.   1

1/211   WORRALL, JOHN. D. of Rochdale, Littleborough, Bacup, Newchurch, Rawtenstall, Todmorden and adjoining townships. Oldham, 1873.   75

1874

1/212   ABBATT, THOMAS. Commercial d. of Bolton, Farnworth, Kearsley, Halliwell, Astley Bridge, Sharples, Turton, and the townships comprised in the Bolton Union. Bolton, 1874.   7,29

1/213   MANNEX, P., & Co. D. of Blackburn, Accrington, Darwen, Chorley and adjacent villages and townships. Preston, 1874.   22

1/214   — D. of Preston, Blackburn, Accrington, Darwen, Chorley, and adjacent villages and townships. Preston, 1874.   6

1/215   MAWDSLEY, J., & SON. Gore's D. of Liverpool and its environs. Liv., 1874.   1

1/216   MORRIS & Co. Commercial d. and gazetteer of Ashton-under-Lyne and district. Nottingham, 1874.   20,29

1/217   — Commercial d. and gazetteer of Cheshire. Nottingham, 1874.   1,59
       Stockport, pp. 599–688.

1/218   SLATER, ISAAC. General and classified d. and street register of Manchester and Salford with their vicinities. Manch., 1874.   1,C

1875

1/219   WORRALL, JOHN. D. of Oldham, Royton, Shaw, Middleton, Lees, Saddleworth, Mossley and adjoining districts. 2nd ed. Oldham, 1875.   11

1875–6

1/220   MANNEX, P., & Co. D. and topography of north-east Lancashire. Preston, 1875–6. 2v.   10(v.1),27(v.2),33(v.2)
       v.1 includes Preston, Blackburn, Accrington, Darwen, Chorley, 1875.
       v.2 includes Bacup, Burnley, Bury, Clitheroe, Colne, Haslingden, Heywood, Radcliffe, Ribchester, Whalley, 1876.

1876

1/221   JOHNSON, ROBERT, & Co. Southport and Birkdale d. Southport, 1876.   16

1/222   MANNEX, P., & Co. History and d. of Barrow-in-Furness, and the whole of North Lonsdale. Preston, 1876.   3,5,RO

1/223   MAWDSLEY, J., & SON. Gore's D. of Liverpool and its environs. Liv., 1876.   1

1/224   SLATER, ISAAC. Royal national commercial d. of Lancashire, and the manufacturing district around Manchester. Manch., 1876.   1,59

1/225   SLATER, ISAAC. Royal national commercial d. of Manchester and Salford, with their vicinities. Manch., 1876.   1,C

1/226   STEWART, A. Name, professional and trade d. of Southport: extract from Slater's Lancashire d., revised and corrected. Southport, 1876.   16

1/227   WORRALL, JOHN. D. of Warrington, Wigan, St. Helens, Widnes, Leigh, Tyldesley, Newton, Earlestown, . . . and adjoining districts. Oldham, 1876.   14,17,34

1876–7

1/228   TILLOTSON & SON. Post Office Bolton d. . . . : together with a suburban d. of the townships in the Bolton Poor Law Union. Bolton, 1876.   7,29

1877

1/229   MANNEX, P., & CO. D. of Preston and district. Preston, 1877.   12,29,72

1877–8

1/230   SLATER, ISAAC. Royal national commercial d. of Manchester and Salford, with their vicinities. Manch., 1877.   1,C

1878

1/231   BARRETT, P., & CO. D. of Blackburn, Accrington, Darwen, Clitheroe . . . and adjacent villages and townships. Preston, 1878.   6

1/232   KELLY & CO. D. of Cheshire. 1878.   1,59

1879

1/233   BARRETT, P., & CO. D. and topography of Blackburn, Burnley, Accrington, Darwen, Colne, Padiham and Nelson, and adjacent villages and townships. Preston, 1879.   9,23

1/234   — D. and topography of Burnley, Colne, Nelson, Padiham. Preston, 1879.   9,23

1/235   MACDONALD & MACDONALD. D. of Rochdale, Milnrow, Littleborough, Bacup, Rossendale, Haslingden, and Todmorden. 1879.   13,21,26,27,50

1/236   MAWDSLEY, J., & SON. Gore's D. of Liverpool and its environs. Liv., 1879.   1

1/237   SLATER, ISAAC. Royal national commercial d. of Lancashire, and the manufacturing district around Manchester. Manch., 1879. 2v.   1,28,59

1/238   — Royal national commercial d. of Manchester and Salford, with their vicinities. Manch., 1879.   1,33,53,C

1880

1/239   BARRETT, P., & CO. D. and topography of Bury, Heywood, Ramsbottom, Radcliffe, Pilkington and adjacent villages and townships. Preston, 1880. 3,10,29

1/240   MANNEX, P., & CO. The d. of Preston and Fylde districts. Preston, 1880. 22

1/241   MAWDSLEY, J., & SON. Gore's D. of Liverpool and its environs. Liv., 1880. 1

1/242   WORRALL, JOHN. Commercial and general d. of Oldham, Royton, Shaw, Middleton, Lees, Saddleworth and adjoining districts. 3rd ed. Oldham, 1880. 3

1881

1/243   AXON, HENRY. Commercial and general d. of Bolton, Farnworth, Kearsley, Halliwell, Astley Bridge, Turton, Ainsworth, Walkden, Westhoughton and the townships comprised in the Bolton Union. Bolton, 1881. 7

1/244   BARRETT, P., & CO. D. of Blackburn, Accrington, Darwen, Clitheroe . . . and adjacent villages and townships. Preston, 1881. 6,RO

1/245   JOHNSON, ROBERT, & CO. Southport and Birkdale d. Southport, 1881. 16

1/246   KELLY & CO. D. of Lancashire, with Liverpool and Manchester. 1881. 1,17

1/247   MANNEX, P., & CO. Topography and d. of Lancaster and sixteen miles round. Preston, 1881. 3,5,28

1/248   MAWDSLEY, J., & SON. Gore's D. of Liverpool and its environs. Liv., 1881. 1,45

1/249   SLATER, ISAAC. Royal national commercial d. of Manchester and Salford, with their vicinities. Manch., 1881. 1,C

1/250   WORRALL, JOHN. Commercial and general d. of Wigan and [places] in the Wigan Union. Oldham, 1881. 18

1/251   — The cotton spinners and manufacturers' d. Oldham, 1881. 29

1881–2

1/252   PORTER, FRANK, (comp.). D. of Oldham and Stalybridge: containing the private and commercial residents (alphabetically arranged) and the trades classified with local intelligence. 1881–2. 11,29

1882

1/253   AXON, HENRY. Commercial annual buyer's guide and street d. for Wigan and adjoining districts. Bolton, 1882. 18

1/254 AXON, HENRY.   Commercial annual street and special
       trades d. for Blackburn, Darwen, Accrington, Oswald-
       twistle, Clitheroe, and adjoining districts. Bolton, 1882.   6

1/255 BARRETT, P., & CO. General and commercial d. of Preston
       and district. Preston, 1882.   3,12,22

1/256 MANNEX, P., & CO. History and d. of Furness and Cartmel.
       Preston, [1882].   1,3,28

1/257 SLATER, ISAAC. Royal national commercial d. of Manchester
       and Salford, with their vicinities. Manch., 1882.   1,C

1882–3

1/258 SLATER, ISAAC. Royal national commercial d. of Southport
       and Birkdale, with their vicinities. Manch., 1882–3.   1,16

1883

1/259 AXON, HENRY. Commercial annual street and special trades
       d. of Blackburn, Darwen, Accrington, Oswaldtwistle,
       Clitheroe and adjoining districts. Bolton, 1883.   6

1/260 BARRETT, P., & CO. D. and topography of Burnley, Colne,
       Nelson, Padiham. Preston, 1883.   9

1/261 — General and commercial d. of Bury, Heywood, Radcliffe,
       Pilkington, Prestwich, Ramsbottom and adjacent villages
       and townships. Preston, 1883.   10,27,50

1/262 MAWDSLEY, J., & SON.   Gore's D. of Liverpool and its
       environs. Liv., 1883.   1

1/263 SLATER, ISAAC. Royal national commercial d. of Cheshire
       and classified trades d. of Liverpool. Manch., 1883.   1,59

1/264 — Royal national commercial d. of Manchester and Salford,
       with their vicinities. Manch., 1883.   1,C

1883–4

1/265 SLATER, ISAAC. D. of Warrington, Widnes, St. Helens,
       Earlestown. Manch., 1883.   14

1/266 — Royal national commercial d. of Southport and Birkdale,
       with their vicinities. Manch., 1883–4.   1,16

1884

1/267 SLATER, ISAAC. Royal national commercial d. of Manchester
       and Salford, with their vicinities. Manch., 1884.   1,C

1/268 WORRALL, JOHN. Commercial and general d. of Oldham,
       Lees, Royton, Shaw, Hollinwood, Saddleworth and
       Mossley, Ashton-under-Lyne, Stalybridge, Dukinfield, and
       the adjoining districts. 4th ed. Oldham, 1884.   11

1/269 — The cotton spinners and manufacturers' d. Oldham,
       1884.   1

1/270 AXON, HENRY. Commercial and general d. of Bolton, Farnworth, Kearsley, Halliwell, Astley Bridge, Horwich, Turton, Ainsworth, Walkden, Westhoughton and the townships comprised in the Bolton Union. 2nd ed. Bolton,
1885.   7

1/271 BARRETT, P., & Co. D. of Blackburn, Accrington, Darwen,
Clitheroe . . . and adjacent villages and townships. Preston,
1885.   6,19

1/272 — General and commercial d. of Preston and district.
Preston, 1885.   12

1/273 MAITLAND, Police Constable. Police Constable Maitland's
Street d. of Bury, with lists of hotels, inns and beer houses.
Bury, 1885.   10

1/274 MAWDSLEY, J., & SON. Gore's D. of Liverpool and its
environs. Liv., 1885.   1

1/275 PORTER, FRANK, (comp.). Postal d. of Bedford-Leigh, Astley,
Atherton, Culcheth, Kenyon, Lowton, Pennington and
Westleigh. Liv., 1885.   54

1/276 — Postal d. of the borough of Wigan, with the adjoining
townships of Abram, Ashton, Aspull, Billinge, Blackrod,
Hindley, Ince, Orrell, Pemberton, Shevington, Standish,
Upholland, Winstanley, Worthington and Wrightington,
with Golborne; containing street, classified trade and
commercial lists. Liv., 1885.   16

1/277 SLATER, ISAAC. Royal national commercial d. of Manchester
and Salford, with their vicinities. Manch., 1885.   C

1/278 WORRALL, JOHN. Commercial d. of Rochdale. Oldham,
1885.   13

1/279 BARRETT, P., & Co. Topography and d. of Lancaster,
Morecambe, Carnforth, Milnthorpe, Kirkby Lonsdale.
Preston, 1886.   28

1/280 — Topography and d. of Preston, the Fylde, Lancaster,
and districts. Preston, 1886.   28

1/281 ROBERTS, J., (comp.). D. of Barrow-in-Furness and the
Furness district. Barrow-in-Furness, 1886.   5

1/282 SLATER, ISAAC. Royal national commercial d. of Manchester
and Salford, with their vicinities. Manch., 1886.   1,C

1/283 — Royal national commercial d. of Southport and Birkdale,
with their vicinities. Manch., 1886.   16

1/284 BLACKBURN & DISTRICT INCORPORATED CHAMBER OF COM-
MERCE. Annual report [and list of members]. Blackburn,
1888.   6

1/285   KELLY & CO. D. of Lancashire with Liverpool and Manchester. 1887.   1,15,17

1/286   — D. of Manchester and suburbs. 1887.   1

1/287   MAWDSLEY, J., & SON. Gore's D. of Liverpool and its environs. Liv., 1887.   1

1/288   MELSOM, R. A. Cheadle [and Northenden] d. 1887.   1,C

1/289   SLATER, ISAAC. Manchester, Salford, and suburban d. Manch., 1887.   1,15

1/290   — Royal national commercial d. of Lancashire and the manufacturing district around Manchester. Manch., [1887]. 2v.   1,17,59

1/291   — Royal national commercial d. of Manchester and Salford with their vicinities. Manch., 1887.   1,25(Eccles only),59

1/292   — Royal national commercial d. of Southport and Birkdale, with their vicinities. Manch., 1887.   16

1/293   SUTTON & CO. D. of St. Helens, Widnes and surrounding district. Manch., 1887.   14

1/294   THOMPSON, HARGREAVES, (comp.). Burnage, Chorlton-cum-Hardy, Didsbury, Fallowfield, and Withington d. Manch., 1887.   1

1/295   — Eccles, Patricroft, Winton, Monton and Barton d. Manch., 1887.   1,25

1/296   TILLOTSON & SON. Post Office Bolton d. . . . : together with a suburban d. of the townships in the Bolton Poor Law Union. Bolton, 1887.   7

1/297   WOODS, E. B. D. of Stockport. Manch. & Stockport, [1887].   59

1/298   WORRALL, JOHN. The cotton spinners and manufacturers' d. Oldham, 1887.   1

1887–8

1/299   SLATER, ISAAC. Royal national commercial d. of Southport and Birkdale, with their vicinities. Manch., 1887–8.   16

1/300   — Royal national commercial d. of Stockport, Heaton Norris and district. Manch., 1888.   59

1/301   SUTTON & CO. D. of Wigan and district. Manch., 1887.   18

1888

1/302   BARRETT, P., & CO. D. of Blackburn, Accrington, Darwen, Clitheroe . . . and adjacent villages and townships. Preston, 1888.   6,19

1/303   BLACKBURN & DISTRICT INCORPORATED CHAMBER OF COMMERCE. Annual report [and list of members]. Blackburn, 1889.   6

1/304 OLDHAM & DISTRICT INCORPORATED CHAMBER OF COM-
MERCE. Annual report [and list of members]. Oldham,
1888.   11

1/305 SLATER, ISAAC.   Manchester, Salford and suburban d.
Manch., 1888.   1,15,25(Eccles only),59,C

1/306 — Royal national commercial d. of Bury, Heywood, Radcliffe, Ramsbottom and districts. Manch., 1888.   1,10,50

1/307 TILLOTSON & SON. Post Office Bolton d. . . . : together with
a suburban d. of the townships in the Bolton Poor Law
Union. Bolton, 1888.   7

1/308 WORRALL, JOHN. Commercial and general d. of Oldham,
Lees, Royton, Shaw, Thornham, Hollinwood, Saddleworth and Mossley: with Ashton-under-Lyne, Stalybridge, Dukinfield and adjoining districts. 5th ed. Old-
ham, 1888.   11

1888–9
1/309 DUNCAN & MILLS. Bury and Radcliffe commercial d.
Bolton, [1888].   10

1/310 — Rochdale and district commercial d. Bolton, 1888.   13,27

1889
1/311 BARRETT, P., & CO. General and commercial d. of Preston
and district. Preston, 1889.   12

1/312 BLACKBURN & DISTRICT INCORPORATED CHAMBER OF COM-
MERCE. Annual report [and list of members]. Blackburn,
1890.   6

1/313 HASLAM & CO. Warrington annual commercial d. Bolton,
1889.   17

1/314 MAWDSLEY, J., & SON. 'Gore's D. of Liverpool and its
environs. Liv., 1889.   1,45

1/315 SLATER, ISAAC.   Manchester, Salford and suburban d.
Manch., 1889.   1,15,C

1/316 WELLS & CO. Lancaster and district d. Shrewsbury, 1889.   28

1/317 WHEWELL, H., & CO. Bolton annual commercial d. [Bolton,
1889].   7

1/318 WORRALL, JOHN. The cotton spinners and manufacturers' d.
Oldham, 1889.   11

1889–90
1/319 TILLOTSON & SON. Chorley d. Bolton, 1889.   22

1/320 WELLS & CO. Lancaster and district d. Shrewsbury, 1889.   28

1890
1/321 BARRETT, P., & CO. D. and topography of Burnley, Colne,
Nelson, Padiham. Preston, 1890.   9,23,32

1/322   BLACKBURN & DISTRICT INCORPORATED CHAMBER OF COMMERCE. Annual report [and list of members]. Blackburn, 1891.   6

1/323   DUNCAN & MILLS. Rochdale and district commercial d. Bolton, 1890.   13

1/324   HASLAM & CO. Wigan, Pemberton and Ince annual commercial d. Bolton, 1890.   18

1/325   MAWDSLEY, J., & SON. Gore's D. of Liverpool and its environs. Liv., 1890.   1

1/326   OLDHAM & DISTRICT INCORPORATED CHAMBER OF COMMERCE. Annual report [and list of members]. Oldham, 1890.   11

1/327   SLATER, ISAAC. Manchester and Salford d. with their vicinities. Manch., 1890.   C

1/328   — Royal national commercial d. of Cheshire and classified trades d. of Liverpool. Manch., 1890.   1

1/329   — Royal national commercial d. of Lancashire and the manufacturing district round Manchester. Manch., 1890.   1
Cheshire, Derbyshire section only.

1/330   — Royal national commercial d. of Southport and Birkdale, with their vicinities. Manch., 1890.   16

1890–1

1/331   TILLOTSON & SON. Post Office Bolton d. . . . : together with a suburban d. of the townships in the Bolton Poor Law Union. Bolton, 1890.   7

1891

1/332   BARRETT, P., & CO. D. of Blackburn, Accrington, Darwen, Clitheroe . . . and adjacent villages and townships. Preston, 1891.   6,19

1/333   BLACKBURN & DISTRICT INCORPORATED CHAMBER OF COMMERCE. Annual report [and list of members]. Blackburn, 1892.   6

1/334   BOTHAM, GEORGE. D. of the postal district of Levenshulme and illustrated family almanack. [1890?].   1

1/335   DUNCAN & MILLS. Blackburn and district d. Bolton, 1891.   6

1/336   KELLY & CO. Post Office d. of Lancashire, Liverpool and Manchester. 1891.   17

1/337   MAWDSLEY, J., & SON. Gore's D. of Liverpool and its environs. Liv., 1891.   1

1/338   OLDHAM & DISTRICT INCORPORATED CHAMBER OF COMMERCE. Annual report [and list of members]. Oldham, 1891.   11

1/339 SLATER, ISAAC. D. of Warrington, Widnes, St. Helens and
Earlestown. [2nd ed.]. Manch., 1891.   17

1/340 — Manchester and Salford d. Manch., 1891.   C
No suburbs.

1/341 — Manchester, Salford and suburban d. Manch., 1891.
1,15,25(Eccles only),C

1/342 — Royal national commercial d. of Lancashire and the
manufacturing district around Manchester. Manch.,
[1890]. 2v.   1

1/343 — Royal national commercial d. of St. Helens and district.
Manch., 1891.   14

1/344 — Royal national commercial d. of Stockport, Heaton
Norris and district. Manch., 1891.   1,59

1/345 WORRALL, JOHN. Commercial and general d. of Oldham,
including Chadderton, Hollinwood, Royton, Shaw,
Thornham, Lees, Springhead and Saddleworth. 6th ed.
Oldham, 1891.   1,11

1/346 — The cotton spinners and manufacturers' d. Oldham,
1891.   1

1891–2

1/347 COLLINSON, RICHARD, (comp.). Manchester Royal Exchange:
d. Manch., [1891].   1

1892

1/348 BARRETT, P., & Co. General and commercial d. of Preston
and district. Preston, 1892.   12,44

1/349 BLACKBURN & DISTRICT INCORPORATED CHAMBER OF COM-
MERCE. Annual report [and list of members]. Blackburn,
1893.   6

1/350 DUNCAN & MILLS. The Bolton and suburban d., embracing
Bolton, Farnworth and Horwich. Bolton, 1891.   7

1/351 KELLY & CO. D. of Cheshire. 1892.   1,59

1/352 MAWDSLEY, J., & SON. Gore's D. of Liverpool and its
environs. Liv., 1892.   1

1/353 OLDHAM & DISTRICT INCORPORATED CHAMBER OF COM-
MERCE. Annual report [and list of members]. Oldham,
1892.   11

1/354 SLATER'S DIRECTORY LTD. Manchester and Salford d.
Manch., 1892.   1

1/355 SLATER, ISAAC. Royal national commercial d. of Lancashire
and the manufacturing district around Manchester.
Manch., [1892]. 2v.   1,59(v.1)

1/356 — Royal national commercial d. of Southport and Birkdale,
with their vicinities. Manch., 1892.   1,16

1/357   WORRALL, JOHN. The cotton spinners and manufacturers' d. Oldham, 1892.   1

1892–3

1/358   TILLOTSON & SON. Post Office Bolton d. . . .: together with a suburban d. of the townships in the Bolton Poor Law Union. Bolton, 1892.   7

1893

1/359   BARRETT, P., & CO. D. and topography of Burnley, Colne, Nelson, Padiham. Preston, 1893.   9,23,32

1/360   BLACKBURN & DISTRICT INCORPORATED CHAMBER OF COM-MERCE. Annual report [and list of members]. Blackburn, 1894.   6

1/361   MAWDSLEY, J., & SON. Gore's D. of Liverpool and its environs. Liv., 1893.   1

1/362   OLDHAM & DISTRICT INCORPORATED CHAMBER OF COM-MERCE. Annual report [and list of members]. Oldham, 1893.   11

1/363   SLATER'S DIRECTORY LTD. Royal national commercial d. of Southport and Birkdale, with their vicinities. Manch., 1893.   1,16

1/364   — Royal national commercial d. of Stockport. Manch., 1893.   1,59

1/365   — & KELLY & CO., LTD. Manchester, Salford and suburban d. 1893.   1,15,59

1893–4

1/366   COLLINSON, RICHARD, (comp.). Manchester Royal Exchange: d. Manch., [1893].   1

1894

1/367   BARRETT, P., & CO. D. of Blackburn, Accrington, Darwen, Clitheroe . . . and adjacent villages and townships. Preston, 1894.   6,19

1/368   BLACKBURN & DISTRICT INCORPORATED CHAMBER OF COM-MERCE. Annual report [and list of members]. Blackburn, 1895.   6

1/369   DUNCAN, J. G. Rochdale and district commercial d. Bolton, 1894.   13

1/370   MAWDSLEY, J., & SON. Gore's D. of Liverpool and its environs. Liv., 1894.   1

1/371   OLDHAM & DISTRICT INCORPORATED CHAMBER OF COMMERCE. Annual report [and list of members]. Oldham, 1894.   11

1/372 SLATER'S DIRECTORY LTD. Royal national commercial d. of
Southport and Birkdale and their vicinities. Manch., 1894.   1,16

1/373 — & KELLY & CO., LTD. Manchester, Salford and suburban
d. 1894.   1,15,59

1/374 WHEWELL, H., & CO. Bolton annual commercial d. Bolton,
1894.   7

1894–5

1/375 JOHNSON, ROBERT, & CO. The "Reliable" d. of Southport
and Birkdale, with Ainsdale, Banks, Blowick, Blundellsands, Churchtown, Crosby, Crossens, Formby, Fresh-
fields, Hightown and Waterloo. Southport, 1894–5.   16

1/376 TILLOTSON & SON. Post Office Bolton d. . . . : together with a
suburban d. of the townships in the Bolton Poor Law
Union. Bolton, 1894.   7

1895

1/377 BARRETT, P., & CO. General and commercial d. of Preston
and district. Preston, 1895.   12

1/378 BLACKBURN & DISTRICT INCORPORATED CHAMBER OF COM-
MERCE. Annual report [and list of members]. Blackburn,
1896.   6

1/379 MAWDSLEY, J., & SON. Gore's D. of Liverpool and its
environs. Liv., 1895.   1

1/380 MORRIS, ERNEST. Sixpenny d. of Chorley. Chorley, 1895.   22

1/381 OLDHAM & DISTRICT INCORPORATED CHAMBER OF COMMERCE.
Annual report [and list of members]. Oldham, 1895.   11

1/382 SLATER'S DIRECTORY LTD. Royal national commercial d. of
Southport and Birkdale, with their vicinities. Manch.,
1895.   1,16

1/383 — D. of Levenshulme, Heaton Chapel, Heaton Mersey,
Heaton Moor, Reddish, Burnage, Withington, Fallowfield and Didsbury. Manch., 1895.   1

1/384 — D. of St. Helens comprising a list of the gentry; and
alphabetical list; register of the principal streets and
classified list of trades. Manch., 1895.   1,14

1/385 — D. of Warrington, Earlestown, Widnes and St. Helens.
Manch., 1895.   1,14,17,34

1/386 — & KELLY & CO., LTD. Manchester, Salford and suburban
d. 1895.   1,15

1/387 — — Royal national d. of Lancashire with Manchester and
Liverpool. Manch. & Liv., 1895.   1,59(v.1)

1/388 WHEWELL, H., & CO. Bolton annual commercial d. Bolton,
1895.   7

1/389   COLLINSON, RICHARD, (comp.). Manchester Royal Exchange: d. Manch., [1895].   1

1896

1/390   BARRETT, P., & CO. D. and topography of Burnley, Colne, Nelson, Padiham. Preston, 1896.   9,23,32

1/391   BLACKBURN & DISTRICT INCORPORATED CHAMBER OF COMMERCE. Annual report [and list of members]. Blackburn, 1897.   6

1/392   COOK, W. J., & CO. D. of Lancaster, Morecambe and district. Boston, 1896.   28

1/393   KELLY & CO. D. of Cheshire. 1896.   59

1/394   MACKERETH, H. W. Mackereth's Third annual Furness year book. Ulverston, [1895].   5

1/395   MAWDSLEY, J., & SON. Gore's D. of Liverpool and its environs. Liv., 1896.   1

1/396   OLDHAM & DISTRICT INCORPORATED CHAMBER OF COMMERCE. Annual report [and list of members]. Oldham, 1896.   11

1/397   SLATER'S DIRECTORY LTD. D. of Eccles, Patricroft, Barton and neighbourhood. Manch., 1896.   25

1/398   — & KELLY & CO., LTD. Manchester, Salford and suburban d. Manch.. 1896.   1,15,59

1896–7

1/399   AINSWORTH, JOHN. North Manchester d.: comprising Cheetham Hill, Crumpsall, (part of) Higher Broughton, Kersal, and (part of) Prestwich. Warrington, [1896].   1

1/400   SLATER'S DIRECTORY LTD. Royal national commercial d. of Southport and Birkdale, with their vicinities. Manch., 1896–7.   1,16

1896–8

1/401   TILLOTSON & SON. Post Office Bolton d. . . .: together with a suburban d. of the townships in the Bolton Poor Law Union. Bolton, 1896.   7

1897

1/402   BARRETT, P., & CO. D. of Blackburn, Accrington, Darwen, Clitheroe . . . and adjacent villages and townships. Preston, 1897.   6,19

1/403   BLACKBURN & DISTRICT INCORPORATED CHAMBER OF COMMERCE. Annual report [and list of members]. Blackburn, 1898.   6

1/404   MACKERETH, H. W. Mackereth's Fourth annual Furness year book. Ulverston, [1896].   5,42

1/405   MAWDSLEY, J., & SON. Gore's D. of Liverpool and its environs. Liv., 1897.   1

1/406   OLDHAM & DISTRICT INCORPORATED CHAMBER OF COMMERCE Annual report [and list of members]. Oldham, 1897.   11

1/407   SLATER'S DIRECTORY LTD. & KELLY & CO., LTD. Manchester, Salford and suburban d. Manch., 1897.   1,15,59

1/408   WORRALL, JOHN. The cotton spinners and manufacturers' d. Oldham, 1897.   1

1898

1/409   BARRETT, P., & CO. General and commercial d. of Preston and district. Preston, 1898.   12

1/410   BLACKBURN & DISTRICT INCORPORATED CHAMBER OF COMMERCE. Annual report [and list of members]. Blackburn, 1899.   6

1/411   KELLY'S DIRECTORIES, LTD. Gore's D. of Liverpool and its environs. 1898.   1

1/412   MACKERETH, H. W. Mackereth's Fifth annual Furness year book. Ulverston, [1897].   5

1/413   OLDHAM & DISTRICT INCORPORATED CHAMBER OF COMMERCE. Annual report [and list of members]. Oldham, 1898.   11

1/414   SLATER'S DIRECTORY LTD. D. of Levenshulme, Heaton Chapel, Heaton Mersey, Heaton Moor, Reddish, Burnage, Withington, Fallowfield and Didsbury. Manch., 1898.   1

1/415   — D. of Prestwich, Eccles, Patricroft, Barton and district, Stretford and Chorlton-cum-Hardy, and neighbourhood. Manch., 1898.   1,52

1/416   — & KELLY'S DIRECTORIES, LTD. D. of Lancashire with Slater's Manchester and Gore's Liverpool. Manch. & Liv., 1898.
County portion only.   1,17

1/417   — — Manchester, Salford and suburban d. Manch., 1898.   1,15,59

1/418   WORRALL, JOHN. The cotton spinners and manufacturers' d. Oldham, 1898.   1

1899

1/419   BARRETT, P., & CO. D. and topography of Burnley, Colne, Nelson, Padiham. Preston, 1899.   9,32

1/420   BLACKBURN & DISTRICT INCORPORATED CHAMBER OF COMMERCE. Annual report [and list of members]. Blackburn, 1900.   1

1/421   BURY TIMES. Street guide and business d. for Bury; also specially compiled historical and other notes on the town and district. Bury, 1899.   10

1/422 COOK, W. J., & Co. D. of Lancaster, Morecambe and district. Derby, 1899.   28

1/423 KELLY'S DIRECTORIES, LTD. Gore's D. of Liverpool and its environs. 1899.   1

1/424 MACKERETH, H. W. Mackereth's Sixth annual Furness year book. Ulverston, [1898].   3,5

1/425 NEW CHESHIRE COUNTY NEWS CO., LTD. The Stockport d. Stockport, [1899].   59

1/426 OLDHAM & DISTRICT INCORPORATED CHAMBER OF COMMERCE. Annual report [and list of members]. Oldham, 1899.   11

1/427 SLATER'S DIRECTORY LTD. D. of Levenshulme, Heaton Chapel, Heaton Mersey, Heaton Moor, Reddish, Burnage, Withington, Fallowfield and Didsbury. Manch., 1899.   1

1/428 — D. of Prestwich, Eccles, Patricroft, Barton and district, Stretford and Chorlton-cum-Hardy, and neighbourhood. Manch., 1899.   1,25

1/429 — & KELLY'S DIRECTORIES, LTD. Manchester, Salford and suburban d. Manch., 1899.   1,25(Eccles only),C

1/430 WATSON, W., & Co. History, topography, general and commercial d. of Lancaster, Morecambe, Skerton, Carnforth, Heysham, Bentham, Bolton-le-Sands, Ellel, Caton, Garstang, Milnthorpe, Kirkby Lonsdale . . . and adjacent villages and townships. Preston, 1899.   28

1/431 WEAVER, THOMAS. The annual d. for the Southport postal district. Southport, 1899.   1,16

1/432 WOODS, E. B. D. of Stockport. Manch., [1899].   59

1/433 WORRALL, JOHN. The cotton spinners and manufacturers' d. Oldham, 1899.   1

1899–1900

1/434 COLLINSON, RICHARD, (comp.). Manchester Royal Exchange: d. Manch., [1899].   1

1/435 DUNCAN, J. G. Rochdale and district commercial and postal d. Bolton, [1899].   13

1899–1901

1/436 TILLOTSON & SON, LTD. Post Office Bolton d. Bolton, 1899.   7

1900

1/437 BARRETT, P., & Co. D. of Blackburn, Accrington, Darwen, Clitheroe . . . and adjacent villages and townships. Preston, 1900.   6

1/438 BLACKBURN & DISTRICT INCORPORATED CHAMBER OF COM-
MERCE. Annual report [and list of members]. Blackburn,
1901. 6

1/439 BULMER, T., & CO. History, topography and d. of Furness
and Cartmel. Preston, [c.1900]. 33

1/440 COOK, W. J., & CO. Blackburn and district (embracing
Fleetwood, Lytham, St. Anne's-on-Sea, and most of the
villages in the Fylde Union) d. 3rd ed. Derby, 1900. 1

1/441 DUNCAN, J. G. Streets and walks, including Duncan's street
d. . . . and local guide, Bolton and district. Bolton, 1900. 7

1/442 KELLY'S DIRECTORIES, LTD. Gore's D. of Liverpool and its
environs. 1900. 1

1/443 MACKERETH, H. W. Mackereth's Seventh annual Furness
year book. Ulverston, [1899]. 3,5

1/444 SLATER'S DIRECTORY LTD. D. of Levenshulme, Heaton
Chapel, Heaton Mersey, Heaton Moor, Reddish, Burnage, Withington, Fallowfield and Didsbury. Manch.,
1900. 1

1/445 — D. of Prestwich, Eccles, Patricroft, Barton and district,
Stretford and Chorlton-cum-Hardy, and neighbourhood.
Manch., 1900. 1,25,C

1/446 — & KELLY'S DIRECTORIES, LTD. Manchester, Salford and
suburban d. Manch., 1900. 1,15,25(Eccles only),59,C

1/447 TOWN & COUNTY DIRECTORIES, LTD. Preston, Barrow and
district trades' d. Manch., 1900. 28

1/448 WEAVER, THOMAS. Annual d. for the Southport postal
district, comprising Ainsdale, Banks, Birkdale, Blowick,
Churchtown, Crossens, Marshside, Martinmere, Parbold
and Newburgh. Southport, 1900. 16

1/449 WHEWELL, H., & CO. Bolton annual commercial d. Bolton,
1900. 7

1/450 WORRALL, JOHN. The cotton spinners and manufacturers'
d. Oldham, 1900. 1

1900–1901

1/451 SLATER'S DIRECTORY LTD. Royal national commercial d. of
Southport and Birkdale, with their vicinities. Manch.,
1900. 1,16

1901

1/452 BARRETT, P., & CO. General and commercial d. of Preston
and district. Preston, 1901. 12

1/453 BLACKBURN & DISTRICT INCORPORATED CHAMBER OF COM-
MERCE. Annual report [and list of members]. Blackburn,
1902. 6

1/454 COLLINSON, RICHARD, (comp.). Manchester Royal Exchange: d. and guide. [1901].   1

1/455 COOK, W. J., & Co. D. of Lancaster, Morecambe and district. Hull, 1901.   1,28

1/456 KELLY'S DIRECTORIES, LTD. D. of Lancashire (exclusive of Manchester and Liverpool). 1901.   1,17,28,59

1/457 — Gore's D. of Liverpool and its environs. 1901.   1

1/458 MACKERETH, H. W. Eighth annual Furness year book. Ulverston, [1900].   3,5,28

1/459 OLDHAM & DISTRICT INCORPORATED CHAMBER OF COMMERCE. Annual report [and list of members]. Oldham, 1901.   11

1/460 SLATER'S DIRECTORY LTD. & KELLY'S DIRECTORIES, LTD. Manchester, Salford and suburban d. Manch., 1901.   1,15,59,C

1902

1/461 BARRETT, P., & Co. D. and topography of Burnley, Colne, Nelson, Padiham. Preston, 1902.   9,23,32

1/462 BLACKBURN & DISTRICT INCORPORATED CHAMBER OF COMMERCE. Annual report [and list of members]. Blackburn, 1903.   6

1/463 COLLINSON, RICHARD, (comp.). Manchester Royal Exchange: d. and guide. Manch., [1902].   1

1/464 KELLY'S DIRECTORIES, LTD. D. of Cheshire. 1902.   1,59

1/465 — Gore's D. of Liverpool and its environs. 1902.   1

1/466 MACKERETH, H. W. Ninth annual Furness year book. Ulverston, [1901].   3,5

1/467 NEW CHESHIRE COUNTY NEWS CO., LTD. The Stockport d. Stockport, 1902.   59

1/468 SLATER'S DIRECTORY LTD. D. of Levenshulme, Heaton Chapel, Heaton Mersey, Heaton Moor, Reddish, Burnage, Withington, Fallowfield and Didsbury. Manch., 1902.   1

1/469 — D. of Prestwich, Eccles, Patricroft, Barton and district, Stretford and Chorlton-cum-Hardy, and neighbourhood. Manch., 1902.   25,C

1/470 — & KELLY'S DIRECTORIES, LTD. Manchester, Salford and suburban d. Manch., 1902.   1,15,C

1/471 WEAVER, THOMAS. The 20th century d. for the Southport postal district. Southport, 1902.   16

1902–04

1/472 TILLOTSON & SON, LTD. Post Office Bolton d. Bolton, 1902.   7

1/472A BARRETT, P., & CO. D. of Blackburn, Accrington, Darwen, Clitheroe . . . and adjacent villages and townships. Preston, 1903.   6,19

1/473 BLACKBURN & DISTRICT INCORPORATED CHAMBER OF COMMERCE. Annual report [and list of members]. Blackburn, 1904.   6

1/474 COLLINSON, RICHARD, (comp.). Manchester Royal Exchange: d. and guide. Manch., [1903].   1

1/475 HOLMES, W. Tenth annual Furness year book. Ulverston, [1902].   3,5

1/476 KELLY'S DIRECTORIES, LTD. Gore's D. of Liverpool and its environs. 1903.   1,8

1/477 PLATT, R. The 20th century d. for the Wigan Union and postal areas. Wigan, 1903.   18

1/478 SLATER'S DIRECTORY LTD. D. of Levenshulme, Heaton Chapel, Heaton Moor, Reddish, Burnage, Withington, Fallowfield and Didsbury. Manch., 1903.   1

1/479 — D. of Prestwich, Eccles, Patricroft, Barton and district, Stretford and Chorlton-cum-Hardy, and neighbourhood. Manch., 1903.   25

1/480 — & KELLY'S DIRECTORIES, LTD. Manchester, Salford and suburban d. Manch., 1903.   1,15,59,C

1/481 WIGAN PRINTING CO. Almanac and street d. Wigan, 1903.   18

1/482 WORRALL, JOHN. The cotton spinners and manufacturers' d. Oldham, 1903.   1

1904

1/483 BARRETT, P., & CO. General and commercial d. of Preston and district. Preston, 1904.   12

1/484 BLACKBURN & DISTRICT INCORPORATED CHAMBER OF COMMERCE. Annual report [and list of members]. Blackburn, 1905.   6

1/485 COLLINSON, RICHARD, (comp). Manchester Royal Exchange: d. and guide. Manch., [1904].   1

1/486 HOLMES, W. Eleventh annual Furness year book. Ulverston, [1903].   3,5

1/487 KELLY'S DIRECTORIES, LTD. Gore's D. of Liverpool and its environs. 1904.   1

1/488 SEED, R., & SONS. Southport and district d. Preston, 1904.   16

1/489 SLATER'S DIRECTORY LTD. D. of Levenshulme, Heaton Chapel, Heaton Mersey, Heaton Moor, Reddish, Burnage, Withington, Fallowfield and Didsbury. Manch., 1904.   RO,C

1/490 SLATER'S DIRECTORY LTD. D. of Prestwich, Eccles, Patricroft, Barton and district, Stretford and Chorlton-cum-
Hardy, and neighbourhood. Manch., 1904.   25

1/491 — & KELLY'S DIRECTORIES, LTD. Manchester, Salford and
suburban d. Manch., 1904.   1,15,59,C

1905

1/492 BARRETT, P., & Co. D. and topography of Burnley, Colne,
Nelson, Padiham. Preston, 1905.   9,32

1/493 BARROW NEWS & MAIL, LTD. Barrow and district year book.
Barrow, [1904].   5

1/494 BLACKBURN & DISTRICT INCORPORATED CHAMBER OF COM-
MERCE. Annual report [and list of members]. Blackburn,
1906.   6

1/495 BURY TIMES. D. of persons occupying houses and shops of a
rental of £15 and upwards per annum in the County
Borough of Bury. Bury, 1905.   10

1/496 COLLINSON, RICHARD, (comp.). Manchester Royal Exchange:
d. and guide. Manch., [1905].   1

1/497 HOLMES, W. Twelfth annual Furness year book. Ulverston,
[1904].   3,5

1/498 KELLY'S DIRECTORIES, LTD. D. of Lancashire (exclusive of
Manchester and Liverpool). 1905. 1,14(St. Helens only),17,28,59

1/499 — Gore's D. of Liverpool and its environs. 1905.   1

1/500 NEW CHESHIRE COUNTY NEWS CO., LTD. The Stockport d.
Stockport, [1905].   59

1/501 SLATER'S DIRECTORY LTD. & KELLY'S DIRECTORIES, LTD.
Manchester, Salford and suburban d. Manch., 1905.
                                                    1,15,59,C

1906

1/502 BARRETT, P., & Co. D. of Blackburn, Accrington, Darwen,
Clitheroe . . . and adjacent villages and townships. Preston, 1906.   6

1/503 BARROW NEWS & MAIL, LTD. Barrow and district year
book. Barrow, [1905].   5

1/504 BLACKBURN & DISTRICT INCORPORATED CHAMBER OF COM-
MERCE. Annual report [and list of members]. Blackburn,
1907.   6

1/505 COLLINSON, RICHARD, (comp.). Manchester Royal Exchange:
d. and guide. Manch., [1906].   1

1/506 EDWARDS, C. P., & Co. Manchester and Salford professional
and trades d. Manch., 1906.   1

1/507 HOLMES, W. Thirteenth annual Furness year book. Ulverston, [1905].   3,5

34

1/508   KELLY'S DIRECTORIES, LTD. D. of Cheshire. 1906.   1,59

1/509   — Gore's D. of Liverpool and its environs. 1906.   1

1/510   RADCLIFFE TIMES. Annual and historical record for Radcliffe, Whitefield and adjoining districts. Radcliffe, 1906.   50

1/511   SEED, R., & SONS. Southport and district d. Preston, 1906.   16

1/512   SLATER'S DIRECTORY LTD. & KELLY'S DIRECTORIES, LTD.
Manchester, Salford and suburban d. Manch., 1906.   1,15,59,C

1907

1/513   BARRETT, P., &. Co. General and commercial d. of Preston
and district. Preston, 1907.   12

1/514   BARROW NEWS & MAIL, LTD. Barrow and district year book.
Barrow, [1906].   5

1/515   BLACKBURN & DISTRICT INCORPORATED CHAMBER OF COM-
MERCE. Annual report [and list of members]. 1908.   6

1/516   BURY TIMES. Bury and Radcliffe annual and district reference book. Bury, 1907.   10

1/517   COLLINSON, RICHARD, (comp.). Manchester Royal Exchange:
d. and guide. Manch., [1907].   1

1/518   HOLMES, W. Fourteenth annual Furness year book. Ulverston, [1906].   3,5

1/519   KELLY'S DIRECTORIES, LTD. Gore's D. of Liverpool and its
environs. 1907.   1

1/520   RADCLIFFE TIMES. Annual and historical record, for Radcliffe, Whitefield and adjoining districts. Radcliffe, 1907.   50

1/521   SLATER'S DIRECTORY LTD. & KELLY'S DIRECTORIES, LTD.
Manchester, Salford and suburban d. Manch., 1907.   1,15,59,C

1/522   TILLOTSON & SON, LTD. Post Office Bolton d. Bolton, 1907.   7

1907–8

1/523   CLEGG, JAMES. Commercial d. of Rochdale. Rochdale,
[1908].   13

1908

1/524   BARRETT, P , & Co. D. and topography of Burnley, Colne,
Nelson, Padiham. Preston, 1908.   9,23

1/525   BARROW NEWS & MAIL, LTD. Barrow and district year book.
Barrow, [1907].   5

1/526   BLACKBURN & DISTRICT INCORPORATED CHAMBER OF COM-
MERCE. Annual report [and list of members]. Blackburn,
1909.   6

1/527   COLLINSON, RICHARD, (comp.). Manchester Royal Exchange:
d. and guide. Manch., [1908].   1

1/528   HOLMES, W. Fifteenth annual Furness year book. Ulverston, [1907].   3,5

1/529   KELLY'S DIRECTORIES, LTD. Gore's D. of Liverpool and its environs. 1908.   1,8

1/530   MACKIE & CO., LTD. Warrington Guardian d. and history of Warrington and environs. Warrington, 1908.   1,17

1/531   RADCLIFFE TIMES. Annual and historical record, for Radcliffe, Whitefield and adjoining districts. Radcliffe, 1908.   50

1/532   SLATER'S DIRECTORY LTD. & KELLY'S DIRECTORIES, LTD. Manchester, Salford and suburban d. Manch., 1908.   1,15,59,C

1/533   TOWN & COUNTY DIRECTORIES, LTD. Liverpool and district trades' d., including Liverpool . . . St. Helens . . . Hindley, Maghull, Newton-le-Willows, Ormskirk, Prescot, Skelmersdale, Southport, Warrington, Widnes, Wigan. Edinburgh, [1908].   1

1/534   WORRALL, JOHN. The cotton spinners and manufacturers' d. Oldham, 1908.   1

1908–9

1/535   EDWARDS, C. P., & CO. Manchester and Salford professional and trades d. Manch., 1908.   1

1/536   SEED, R., & SONS. Southport and district d.: including Ainsdale, Banks, Birkdale, Blowick, Churchtown, Crossens, Formby, Freshfield and Marshside. Preston, 1908.   1,16

1909

1/537   BARRETT, P., & CO. D. of Blackburn, Accrington, Darwen, Clitheroe . . . and adjacent villages and townships. Preston, 1909.   6,19

1/538   BARROW NEWS & MAIL, LTD. Barrow and district year book. Barrow, [1908].   5

1/539   BLACKBURN & DISTRICT INCORPORATED CHAMBER OF COMMERCE. Annual report [and list of members]. Blackburn, 1910.   6

1/540   COLLINSON, RICHARD, (comp.). Manchester Royal Exchange: d. and guide. Manch., [1909].   1

1/541   HOLMES, W. Sixteenth annual Furness year book. Ulverston, [1908].   3,5

1/542   KELLY'S DIRECTORIES, LTD. D. of Lancashire (exclusive of the cities of Manchester and Liverpool). 1909.   1,17,19,59

1/543   — Gore's D. of Liverpool and its environs. 1909.   1,45

1/544   RADCLIFFE TIMES. Annual and historical record for Radcliffe, Whitefield and adjoining districts. Radcliffe, 1909.   50

1/545   SLATER'S DIRECTORY LTD. & KELLY'S DIRECTORIES, LTD.
Manchester, Salford and suburban d. Manch., 1909.   1,15,59,C

1/546   WORRALL, JOHN. The cotton spinners and manufacturers' d.
Oldham, 1909.   1

1909–10

1/547   SEED, R., & SONS. Wigan and district d. including Pember-
ton, Hindley, Ince, Abram, Appley Bridge, Ashton-in-
Makerfield, Gathurst, Haigh, Orrell, Parbold, Shevington,
Standish, Upholland. Preston, 1909.   1,18

1910

1/548   BARRETT, P., & CO. General and commercial d. of Preston
and district. Preston, 1910.   12

1/549   BARROW NEWS & MAIL, LTD. Barrow and district year book.
Barrow, [1909].   5

1/550   BLACKBURN & DISTRICT INCORPORATED CHAMBER OF COM-
MERCE. Annual report [and list of members]. Blackburn,
1911.   6

1/551   COLLINSON, RICHARD, (comp.). Manchester Royal Exchange:
d. and guide. Manch., [1910].   1

1/552   KELLY'S DIRECTORIES, LTD. D. of Cheshire. 1910.   1,59

1/553   — Gore's D. of Liverpool and its environs. 1910.   1

1/554   NEW CHESHIRE COUNTY NEWS CO., LTD. The Stockport and
Hazel Grove d. Stockport, 1910.   1,59

1/555   RADCLIFFE TIMES. Annual and historical record for Radcliffe, Whitefield and adjoining districts. Radcliffe, 1910.   50

1/556   SLATER'S DIRECTORY LTD. & KELLY'S DIRECTORIES, LTD.
Manchester, Salford and suburban d. Manch., 1910.   1,15,59,C

1/557   WORRALL, JOHN, LTD. The cotton spinners and manufacturers' d. Oldham, 1910.   1,11

1910–11

1/558   EDWARDS, C. P., & CO. Manchester and Salford professional
and trades d. Manch., 1910.   1

1/559   SEED, R., & SONS. Southport and district d. Preston, 1910.   16

1911

1/560   BARRETT, P., & CO. D. and topography of Burnley, Colne,
Nelson, Padiham. Preston, 1911   9,23

1/561   BARROW NEWS & MAIL, LTD. Barrow and district year book.
Barrow, [1910].   5

1/562   BLACKBURN & DISTRICT INCORPORATED CHAMBER OF COM-
MERCE. Annual report [and list of members]. Blackburn,
1912.   6

1/563   Bulmer, T., & Co. History, topography and d. of Furness
and Cartmel. 2nd ed. Preston, 1911.   3,5,RO

1/564   Collinson, Richard, (comp.). Manchester Royal Exchange:
d. and guide. Manch., [1911].   1

1/565   Kelly's Directories, Ltd. Gore's D. of Liverpool and its
environs. 1911.   1

1/566   Radcliffe Times. Annual historical record for Radcliffe,
Whitefield and adjoining districts. Radcliffe, 1911.   50

1/567   Slater's Directory Ltd. & Kelly's Directories, Ltd.
Manchester, Salford and suburban d. Manch., 1911.   1,15,59,C

1/568   Tillotson & Son, Ltd. Post Office Bolton d. Bolton, 1911.   1,7

1/569   Worrall, John, Ltd. The cotton spinners and manufacturers' d. Oldham, 1911.   1

1912

1/570   Barrett, P., & Co. D. of Blackburn, Accrington, Darwen,
Clitheroe . . . and adjacent villages and townships. Preston, 1912.   19

1/571   Barrow News & Mail, Ltd. Barrow and district year book.
Barrow, [1911].   5

1/572   Blackburn & District Incorporated Chamber of Commerce. Annual report [and list of members]. Blackburn,
1913.   6

1/573   Bulmer, T., & Co. History, topography and d. of Lancaster
and district. Preston, [1912].   3,28,C,RO

1/574   Bury Times. Bury and Radcliffe annual and district reference book . . . Bury, 1912.   10

1/575   Collinson, Richard, (comp.). Manchester Royal Exchange:
d. and guide. Manch., [1912].   1

1/576   Fletcher & Speight, Ltd. The Bury commercial almanack
and corporation manual. Bury, [1912].   10

1/577   Kelly's Directories, Ltd. Gore's D. of Liverpool and its
environs. 1912.   1,45

1/578   Radcliffe Times. Annual and historical record for Radcliffe, Whitefield and adjoining districts. Radcliffe, 1912.   50

1/579   Slater's Directory Ltd. & Kelly's Directories, Ltd.
Manchester, Salford and suburban d. Manch., 1912.   1,15,59,C

1/580   Worrall, John, Ltd. The cotton spinners and manufacturers' d. Oldham, 1912.   1

1912–13

1/581   Seed, R., & Sons. Southport and district d. Preston, 1912.   1,16

1913

1/582   BARRETT, P., & CO. General and commercial d. of Preston and district. Preston, 1913.   12

1/583   BARROW NEWS & MAIL, LTD. Barrow and district year book. Barrow, [1912].   5

1/584   BLACKBURN & DISTRICT INCORPORATED CHAMBER OF COMMERCE. Annual report [and list of members]. Blackburn, 1914.   6

1/585   BULMER, T., & CO. History, topography and d. of Lancaster and district. Ed. by J. Bulmer. Preston, [1913].   28,RO

1/586   BURY TIMES. Bury and Radcliffe annual and district reference book. Bury, 1913.   10

1/587   COLLINSON, RICHARD, (comp.). Manchester Royal Exchange: d. and guide. Manch., [1913].   1

1/588   KELLY'S DIRECTORIES, LTD. D. of Lancashire (exclusive of the cities of Manchester and Liverpool). 1913.   1,17,28,59,C

1/589   — Gore's D. of Liverpool and its environs. 1913.   1,C

1/590   RADCLIFFE TIMES. Annual and historical record for Radcliffe, Whitefield and adjoining districts. Radcliffe, 1913.   50

1/591   SLATER'S DIRECTORY LTD. & KELLY'S DIRECTORIES, LTD. Manchester, Salford and suburban d. Manch., 1913.   1,15,59,C

1/592   WENTWORTH PUBLISHING CO. Waterloo, Blundellsands, Great Crosby and Seaforth d. Liv., 1913.   45
     Includes Hightown, Ince Blundell, Little Crosby, Lunt, Netherton and Sefton.

1/593   WORRALL, JOHN, LTD. The cotton spinners and manufacturers' d. Oldham, 1913.   1

1914

1/594   BARRETT, P., & CO. D. and topography of Burnley, Colne, Nelson, Padiham. Preston, 1914.   9,23

1/595   BARROW NEWS & MAIL, LTD. Barrow and district year book. Barrow, [1913].   5

1/596   BLACKBURN & DISTRICT INCORPORATED CHAMBER OF COMMERCE. Annual report [and list of members]. Blackburn, 1915.   6

1/597   COLLINSON, RICHARD, (comp.). Manchester Royal Exchange: d. and guide. Manch., [1914].   1

1/598   FLETCHER & SPEIGHT, LTD. The " F. & S." Bury annual, almanack and business d. Bury, [1914].   10

1/599   KELLY'S DIRECTORIES, LTD. D. of Cheshire. 1914.   1,59

1/600   — Gore's D. of Liverpool and its environs. 1914.   1

1/601   MANCHESTER COAL EXCHANGE. D. Manch., [1914].   1

1/602　SLATER'S DIRECTORY LTD. & KELLY'S DIRECTORIES, LTD. Manchester, Salford and suburban d. Manch., 1914.　1,15,59,C

1/603　WORRALL, JOHN, LTD. The cotton spinners and manufacturers' d. Oldham, 1914.　1

1914–15

1/604　COPE, E. F., & CO. Cheshire d. and buyers' guide. Walsall, [1914].　1AS
　　　Stockport and district, pp. 145–186.

1/605　SEED, R., & SONS. Southport and district d. Preston, 1914.　1,16

1/606　THOMPSON, H. Street register d. of . . . householders in Southport, Birkdale and Ainsdale, their telephone numbers and other particulars. Southport, [1914].　16,29

1915

1/607　BARRETT, P., & CO. D. of Blackburn, Accrington, Darwen, Clitheroe . . . and adjacent villages and townships. Preston, 1915.　6,19

1/608　BARROW NEWS & MAIL, LTD. Barrow and district year book. Barrow, [1914].　5

1/609　BLACKBURN & DISTRICT INCORPORATED CHAMBER OF COMMERCE. Annual report [and list of members]. Blackburn, 1916.　6

1/610　COLLINSON, RICHARD, (comp.). Manchester Royal Exchange: d. and guide. Manch., [1915].　1

1/611　FLETCHER & SPEIGHT, LTD. The "F. & S." Bury annual, almanack and business d. Bury, [1915].　10

1/612　KELLY'S DIRECTORIES, LTD.　Gore's D. of Liverpool and its environs. 1915.　1,79

1/613　PORTER, FRANK, (comp.). Postal d. of the county borough of Bootle with Orrell and Litherland added, containing street list, alphabetical and trades lists, and name, occupation and address of every householder. Liv., 1915.　8

1/614　SLATER'S DIRECTORY LTD. & KELLY'S DIRECTORIES, LTD. Manchester, Salford and suburban d. Manch., 1915.　1,15,59,C

1/615　WORRALL, JOHN, LTD. The cotton spinners and manufacturers' d. Oldham, 1915.　1,11

1916

1/616　BARROW NEWS & MAIL, LTD. Barrow and district year book. Barrow, [1915].　5

1/617　BLACKBURN & DISTRICT INCORPORATED CHAMBER OF COMMERCE. Annual report [and list of members]. Blackburn, 1917.　6

1/618   CLEGG, JAMES.   Commercial d. of Rochdale, Milnrow, Norden, Wardle, Whitworth, Littleborough, and adjoining townships. Rochdale, 1916.   1,3,13

1/619   COLLINSON, RICHARD, LTD., (comp.).   Manchester Royal Exchange: d. and guide. Manch., [1916].   1

1/620   FLETCHER & SPEIGHT, LTD. The "F. & S." Bury annual, almanack and business d. Bury, 1916.   10

1/621   KELLY'S DIRECTORIES, LTD. Gore's D. of Liverpool and its environs. 1916.   1

1/622   SLATER'S DIRECTORY LTD. & KELLY'S DIRECTORIES, LTD. Manchester, Salford and suburban d. Manch., 1916.   1,15,59,C

1/623   WORRALL, JOHN, LTD. The cotton spinners and manufacturers' d. Oldham, 1916.   1

1917

1/624   BARRETT, P., & CO. General and commercial d. of Preston and district. Preston, 1917.   12

1/625   BARROW NEWS & MAIL, LTD. Barrow and district year book. Barrow, [1916].   5

1/626   BLACKBURN & DISTRICT INCORPORATED CHAMBER OF COMMERCE. Annual report [and list of members]. Blackburn, 1918.   6

1/627   COLLINSON, RICHARD, LTD., (comp.).   Manchester Royal Exchange: d. and guide. Manch., [1917].   1

1/628   KELLY'S DIRECTORIES, LTD. Gore's D. of Liverpool and its environs. 1917.   1

1/629   SLATER'S DIRECTORY LTD. & KELLY'S DIRECTORIES, LTD. Manchester, Salford and suburban d. Manch., 1917.   1,15,59,C

1/630   WORRALL, JOHN, LTD. The cotton spinners and manufacturers' d. Oldham, 1917.   11

1918

1/631   BARROW NEWS & MAIL, LTD. Barrow and district year book. Barrow, [1917].   5

1/632   BLACKBURN & DISTRICT INCORPORATED CHAMBER OF COMMERCE. Annual report [and list of members]. Blackburn, 1919.   6

1/633   COLLINSON, RICHARD, LTD., (comp.).   Manchester Royal Exchange: d. and guide. Manch., [1918].   1

1/634   KELLY'S DIRECTORIES, LTD. D. of Lancashire (exclusive of the cities of Manchester and Liverpool). 1918.   1,59,C

1/635   — Gore's D. of Liverpool and its environs. 1918.   1

1/636   SLATER'S DIRECTORY LTD. & KELLY'S DIRECTORIES, LTD. Manchester, Salford and suburban d. Manch., 1918.   1,15,59,C

1/637　Worrall, John, Ltd. The cotton spinners and manufacturers' d. Oldham, 1918.　　　1

1919

1/638　Blackburn & District Incorporated Chamber of Commerce. Annual report [and list of members]. Blackburn, 1920.　　　6

1/639　Kelly's Directories, Ltd. Gore's D. of Liverpool and its environs. 1919.　　　1

1/640　Manchester Coal Exchange. D. Manch., [1919].　　　1

1/641　Preston & District Incorporated Chamber of Commerce. Fourth annual report, statement of accounts and list of members. Preston, 1920.　　　12

1/642　Slater's Directory Ltd. & Kelly's Directories, Ltd. Manchester, Salford and suburban d. Manch., 1919.　　　1,15,C

1920

1/643　Barrow News & Mail, Ltd. Barrow and district year book. Barrow, [1919].　　　5

1/644　Blackburn & District Incorporated Chamber of Commerce. Annual report [and list of members]. Blackburn, 1921.　　　6

1/645　Collinson, Richard, Ltd., (comp.). Manchester Royal Exchange: d. and guide. Manch., [1920].　　　1

1/646　Kelly's Directories, Ltd. Gore's D. of Liverpool and its environs. 1920.　　　1

1/647　Preston & District Incorporated Chamber of Commerce. Fifth annual report, statement of accounts and list of members. Preston, 1921.　　　12

1/648　Slater's Directory Ltd. & Kelly's Directories, Ltd. Manchester, Salford and suburban d. Manch., 1920.　　　1,15,59,C

1/649　Worrall, John, Ltd. The cotton spinners and manufacturers' d. Oldham, 1920.　　　1,29

1920–21

1/650　Southport Visiter. D. of Southport . . . Southport, 1920.　　　16

1921

1/651　Blackburn & District Incorporated Chamber of Commerce. Annual report [and list of members]. Blackburn, 1922.　　　6

1/652　Collinson, Richard, Ltd.,(comp.). Manchester Royal Exchange: d. and guide. Manch., [1921].　　　1

1/653　Cope, E. F., & Co. Bolton and district d. and buyers' guide. Walsall, 1921.　　　7

1/654   GENERAL POST OFFICE. [Telephone d. for] Manchester and south-east Lancashire district (including Rochdale). May, 1921.   1

1/655   — [Telephone d. for] mid-Lancashire district (including Blackburn, Bolton and Preston). May, 1921.   1

1/656   KELLY'S DIRECTORIES, LTD. Gore's D. of Liverpool and its environs. 1921.   1

1/657   PRESTON & DISTRICT INCORPORATED CHAMBER OF COMMERCE. Sixth annual report, statement of accounts and list of members. Preston, 1922.   12

1/658   SLATER'S DIRECTORY LTD. & KELLY'S DIRECTORIES, LTD. Manchester, Salford and suburban d. Manch., 1921.   1,15,59,C

1/659   WORRALL, JOHN, LTD. The cotton spinners and manufacturers' d. Oldham, 1921.   1

1922

1/660   BARRETT, P., & CO. General and commercial d. of Preston and district. Preston, 1922.   12

1/661   BARROW NEWS & MAIL, LTD. Barrow and district year book. Barrow, [1921].   5

1/662   BLACKBURN & DISTRICT INCORPORATED CHAMBER OF COMMERCE. Annual report [and list of members]. Blackburn, 1923.   6

1/663   COLLINSON, RICHARD, LTD., (comp.). Manchester Royal Exchange: d. and guide. Manch., [1922].   1

1/664   COPE, E. F., & CO. Bolton and district d. and buyers' guide. Walsall, 1922.   7

1/665   GENERAL POST OFFICE. [Telephone d. for] Manchester and south-east Lancashire district (including Rochdale). May and November, 1922.   1

1/666   — [Telephone d. for] mid-Lancashire district (including Blackburn, Bolton and Preston). May and November, 1922.   1

1/667   KELLY'S DIRECTORIES, LTD. Gore's D. of Liverpool and its environs. 1922.   1

1/668   — Slater's D. of Manchester, Salford and suburbs. 1922.   1,15,C

1/669   MANCHESTER COAL EXCHANGE. D. Manch., [1922].   1

1/670   PRESTON & DISTRICT INCORPORATED CHAMBER OF COMMERCE. Seventh annual report, statement of accounts and list of members. Preston, 1923.   12

1/671   TILLOTSON & SON, LTD. Post Office Bolton d. Bolton, 1922.   7

1/672   WORRALL, JOHN, LTD. The cotton spinners and manufacturers' d. Oldham, 1922.   1

1923

1/673   BARRETT, P., & CO. D. and topography of Burnley, Colne, Nelson, Padiham. Preston, 1923.   9,32

1/674   BLACKBURN & DISTRICT INCORPORATED CHAMBER OF COMMERCE. Annual report [and list of members]. Blackburn, 1924.   6

1/675   COLLINSON, RICHARD, LTD., (comp.). Manchester Royal Exchange: d. and guide. Manch., [1923].   1

1/676   GENERAL POST OFFICE. [Telephone d. for] Manchester and south-east Lancashire district (including Rochdale). June and December, 1923.   1

1/677   — [Telephone d. for] mid-Lancashire district (including Blackburn, Bolton and Preston). June and December, 1923.   1

1/678   KELLY'S DIRECTORIES, LTD. D. of Cheshire. 1923.   1,59

1/679   — Gore's D. of Liverpool and its environs. 1923.   1

1/680   — Slater's D. of Manchester, Salford and suburbs. 1923.   1,15,59,C

1/681   PRESTON & DISTRICT INCORPORATED CHAMBER OF COMMERCE. Eighth annual report, statement of accounts and list of members. Preston, 1924.   12

1/682   TOWN & COUNTY DIRECTORIES, LTD. Liverpool and district trades d. Edinburgh, 1923.   48

1/683   WORRALL, JOHN, LTD. The cotton spinners and manufacturers' d. Oldham, 1923.   1,11

1924

1/684   BARROW NEWS & MAIL, LTD. The Furness and district year book and d. Barrow, [1924].   3,5

1/685   BLACKBURN & DISTRICT INCORPORATED CHAMBER OF COMMERCE. Annual report [and list of members]. Blackburn, 1925.   6

1/686   COLLINSON, RICHARD, LTD., (comp.). Manchester Royal Exchange: d. and guide. Manch., [1924].   1

1/687   GENERAL POST OFFICE. [Telephone d. for] Manchester and south-east Lancashire district (including Rochdale). June and December, 1924.   1

1/688   KELLY'S DIRECTORIES, LTD. D. of Lancashire. 1924. 1,3,11(Oldham only),17,18(Wigan only),44(Fleetwood only),50, 59,C

1/689   — Gore's D. of Liverpool and its environs. 1924.   1

1/690   — Slater's D. of Manchester, Salford and suburbs. 1924.   1,15,59,C

1/691   MANCHESTER COAL EXCHANGE. D. Manch., [1924].   1

1/692   PRESTON & DISTRICT INCORPORATED CHAMBER OF COMMERCE. Ninth annual report, statement of accounts and list of members. Preston, 1925.   12

1/693   WORRALL, JOHN, LTD. The cotton spinners and manufacturers' d. Oldham, 1924.   1

1924–5

1/694   SEED, R., & SONS. Southport and district d. Preston, 1924.   1,16

1/695   SOUTHPORT VISITER. D. of Southport. Southport, 1924.   16

1925

1/696   BARRETT, P., & CO. D. of Blackburn, Accrington, Darwen, Clitheroe . . . and adjacent villages and townships. Preston, 1925.   6,19

1/697   BARROW NEWS & MAIL, LTD. Furness and district year book and d. Barrow, [1925].   5

1/698   BLACKBURN & DISTRICT INCORPORATED CHAMBER OF COMMERCE. Annual report [and list of members]. Blackburn, 1926.   6

1/699   COLLINSON, RICHARD, LTD., (comp.). Manchester Royal Exchange: d. and guide. Manch., [1925].   1

1/700   COPE, E. F., & CO. Bolton and district d. and buyers' guide. Walsall, 1925.   7

1/701   GENERAL POST OFFICE. [Telephone d. for] Manchester and south-east Lancashire district (including Rochdale). June and December, 1925.   1

1/702   KELLY'S DIRECTORIES, LTD. Gore's D. of Liverpool and its environs. 1925.   1,45

1/703   — Slater's D. of Manchester, Salford and suburbs. 1925.   1,15,59,C

1/704   PRESTON & DISTRICT INCORPORATED CHAMBER OF COMMERCE. Tenth annual report, statement of accounts and list of members. Preston, 1926.   12

1/705   WENTWORTH PUBLISHING CO. Waterloo, Blundellsands, Great Crosby and Seaforth d. Liv., 1925.   45
     Includes also Hightown, Ince Blundell, Little Crosby, Lunt, Netherton, Sefton and Thornton.

1/706   WORRALL, JOHN, LTD. The cotton spinners and manufacturers' d. Oldham, 1925.   1

1925–6

1/707   SEED, R., & SONS. Wigan and district d. Preston, 1925.   1,18

1926

1/708   BARRETT, P., & CO. General and commercial d. of Preston and district. Preston, 1926.   3,12

1/709   BARROW NEWS & MAIL, LTD.   Furness and district year book and d. Barrow, [1926].   5

1/710   BLACKBURN & DISTRICT INCORPORATED CHAMBER OF COMMERCE. Annual report [and list of members]. Blackburn, 1927.   6

1/711   COLLINSON, RICHARD, LTD., (comp.).   Manchester Royal Exchange: d. and guide. Manch., [1926].   1

1/712   GENERAL POST OFFICE. [Telephone d. for] Manchester and south-east Lancashire district (including Rochdale). June and December, 1926.   1

1/713   KELLY'S DIRECTORIES, LTD.   Gore's D. of Liverpool and its environs. 1926.   1

1/714   — Slater's D. of Manchester, Salford and suburbs. 1926. 1,15,59,C

1/715   PRESTON & DISTRICT INCORPORATED CHAMBER OF COMMERCE. Eleventh annual report, statement of accounts and list of members. Preston, 1927.   12

1/716   WORRALL, JOHN, LTD. The cotton spinners and manufacturers' d. Oldham, 1926.   1

1926–7

1/717   COPE, E. F., & CO. Oldham, Rochdale and district d. and buyers' guide. Walsall, 1926.   11

1927

1/718   BARROW NEWS & MAIL, LTD. The Furness and district year book and d. Barrow, [1927].   3,5

1/719   BLACKBURN & DISTRICT INCORPORATED CHAMBER OF COMMERCE. Annual report [and list of members]. Blackburn, 1928.   6

1/720   COLLINSON, RICHARD, LTD., (comp.).   Manchester Royal Exchange: d. and guide. Manch., [1927].   1

1/721   GENERAL POST OFFICE. [Telephone d. for] Manchester and south-east Lancashire district (including Rochdale). June and December, 1927.   1

1/722   KELLY'S DIRECTORIES, LTD.   Gore's D. of Liverpool and its environs. 1927.   1

1/723   — Slater's D. of Manchester, Salford and suburbs. 1927.   1,15,59,C

1/724   MANCHESTER COAL EXCHANGE. D. Manch., [1927].   1

1/725   PRESTON & DISTRICT INCORPORATED CHAMBER OF COMMERCE. Twelfth annual report, statement of accounts and list of members. Preston, 1928.   1,12

1/726   TILLOTSON & SON, LTD. Post Office Bolton d. Bolton, 1927.   7

1/727   WORRALL, JOHN, LTD. The cotton spinners and manufacturers' d. Oldham, 1927.   1

1/728 BARRETT, P., & CO. D. and topography of Burnley, Colne, Nelson, Padiham. Preston, 1927. 9

1/729 SEED, R., & SON. Southport and district d. Preston, 1927. 1,16

1928

1/730 AUBREY & CO. D. of Cheshire. 1928. 59

1/731 BARROW NEWS & MAIL, LTD. Furness and district year book and d. Barrow, [1928]. 5

1/732 BLACKBURN & DISTRICT INCORPORATED CHAMBER OF COMMERCE. Annual report [and list of members]. Blackburn, 1929. 6

1/733 COLLINSON, RICHARD, LTD., (comp.). Manchester Royal Exchange: d. and guide. Manch., [1928]. 1

1/734 COPE, E. F., & CO. Bolton and district d. and buyers' guide. Walsall, 1928. 7

1/735 GENERAL POST OFFICE. [Telephone d. for] Manchester and south-east Lancashire district (including Rochdale). June and December, 1928. 1

1/736 KELLY'S DIRECTORIES, LTD. D. of Cheshire. 1928. 1,59

1/737 — Gore's D. of Liverpool and its environs. 1928. 1

1/738 — Slater's D. of Manchester, Salford and suburbs. 1928. 1,15,59,C

1/739 PRESTON & DISTRICT INCORPORATED CHAMBER OF COMMERCE. Thirteenth annual report, statement of accounts and list of members. Preston, 1929. 1,12

1/740 WORRALL, JOHN, LTD. The cotton spinners and manufacturers' d. Oldham, 1928. 1

1928–9

1/741 COPE, E. F., & CO. Oldham, Rochdale and district d. and buyers' guide. Walsall, 1928. 13

1929

1/742 BARRETT, P., & CO. General and commercial d. of Blackpool and the Fylde. Preston, 1929. 3

1/743 BARROW NEWS & MAIL, LTD. The Furness and district year book and d. Barrow, [1929]. 3,5

1/744 BLACKBURN & DISTRICT INCORPORATED CHAMBER OF COMMERCE. Annual report [and list of members]. Blackburn, 1930. 6

1/745 COLLINSON, RICHARD, LTD., (comp.). Manchester Royal Exchange: d. and guide. Manch., [1929]. 1

1/746   COPE, E. F., & CO. Preston, Blackpool and district d. and
buyers' guide. Walsall, 1929.   28

1/747   GENERAL POST OFFICE. [Telephone d. for] Manchester and
south-east Lancashire district (including Rochdale).
June and December, 1929.   1

1/748   KELLY'S DIRECTORIES, LTD. Gore's D. of Liverpool and its
environs. 1929.   1

1/749   — Slater's D. of Manchester, Salford and suburbs. 1929.
    1,3,15,59,C

1/750   MANCHESTER COAL EXCHANGE. D. Manch., [1929].   1

1/751   PRESTON & DISTRICT INCORPORATED CHAMBER OF COM-
MERCE. Fourteenth annual report, statement of accounts
and list of members. Preston, 1930.   12

1/752   WENTWORTH PUBLISHING CO. Waterloo, Blundellsands,
Great Crosby, and Seaforth d. Liv., 1929.   45
    Includes also Hightown, Ince Blundell, Little Crosby, Lunt,
Netherton, Sefton and Thornton.

1/753   WORRALL, JOHN, LTD. The cotton spinners and manufacturers' d. Oldham, 1929.   1

1929–30

1/754   BURY & DISTRICT CHAMBER OF COMMERCE. Annual report
and list of members. Bury, 1930.   1

1930

1/755   BARRETT, P., & CO. D. of Blackburn, Accrington, Darwen,
Clitheroe . . . and adjacent villages and townships. Preston, 1930.   6,19,RO

1/756   BARROW NEWS & MAIL, LTD. The Furness and district year
book and d. Barrow, [1930].   3,5

1/757   BLACKBURN & DISTRICT INCORPORATED CHAMBER OF COM-
MERCE. Annual report [and list of members]. Blackburn,
1931.   6

1/758   COLLINSON, RICHARD, LTD., (comp.). Manchester Royal
Exchange: d. and guide. Manch., [1930].   1

1/759   COLNE CHAMBER OF TRADE. Shopping list and book of
information. Colne, [1930?].   23

1/760   COPE, E. F., & CO. Bolton and district d. and buyers' guide.
Walsall, 1930.   7

1/761   COULTON & CO. Street d. for Colne, Nelson and Barrowford. Nelson, [1930].   23

1/762   GENERAL POST OFFICE. [Telephone d. for] Manchester and
south-east Lancashire district (including Rochdale).
June and December, 1930.   1

1/763   KELLY'S DIRECTORIES, LTD.   Gore's D. of Liverpool and its environs. 1930.   1

1/764   — Slater's D. of Manchester, Salford and suburbs. 1930.   1,15,59,C

1/765   MANCHESTER COAL EXCHANGE. D. Manch., [1930].   1

1/767   OLDHAM & DISTRICT INCORPORATED CHAMBER OF COMMERCE. Annual report [and list of members]. Oldham, [1931].   1

1/768   WORRALL, JOHN, LTD. The cotton spinners and manufacturers' d. Oldham, 1930.   1

1930–1

1/769   BURY & DISTRICT CHAMBER OF COMMERCE. Annual report and list of members. Bury, 1931.   1

1/770   SEED, R., & SONS. Southport and district d. Preston, 1930.   1,16

1/771   TOWN & COUNTY DIRECTORIES, LTD. Preston, Barrow and district trades' d. Edinburgh, 1930.   28

1931

1/772   BARROW NEWS & MAIL, LTD. The Furness and district year book and d. Barrow, [1931].   3,5

1/773   BLACKBURN & DISTRICT INCORPORATED CHAMBER OF COMMERCE. Annual report [and list of members]. Blackburn, 1932.   1

1/774   COPE, E. F., & CO. Preston, Blackpool and district d. and buyers' guide. Walsall, 1931.   28

1/775   GENERAL POST OFFICE. [Telephone d. for] Manchester and south-east Lancashire district (including Rochdale). June and December, 1931.   1

1/776   KELLY'S DIRECTORIES, LTD. Gore's D. of Liverpool and its environs. 1931.   1

1/777   — Slater's D. of Manchester, Salford and suburbs. 1931.   1,15,59,C

1/778   LIVERPOOL ORGANIZATION FOR ADVANCING THE INTERESTS OF MERSEYSIDE. D. of Merseyside manufacturers. Liv., [1931].   1,8,17,34,79

1/779   OLDHAM & DISTRICT INCORPORATED CHAMBER OF COMMERCE. Annual report [and list of members]. Oldham, [1932].   1

1/780   PRESTON & DISTRICT INCORPORATED CHAMBER OF COMMERCE. Sixteenth annual report, statement of accounts and list of members. Preston, 1932.   1,12

1/781   WORRALL, JOHN, LTD. The Lancashire textile industry. Oldham, 1931.   1

1/782   BURY & DISTRICT CHAMBER OF COMMERCE. Annual report and list of members. Bury, 1932.   1

1/783   COPE, E. F., & CO. Oldham, Rochdale and district d. and buyers' guide. Walsall, 1931.   11

1/784   COX, F. J. Liverpool and Manchester commercial agents' d. and handbook of Lancashire trade. Liv., [1931].   1

1/785   TOWN & COUNTY DIRECTORIES, LTD. Preston, Barrow and district trades' d. Edinburgh, 1931.   28

1932

1/786   AUBREY & CO. Lancashire d. Walsall, 1932.   28

1/787   BARRETT, P., & CO. General and commercial d. of Preston and district. Preston, 1932.   3,12

1/788   BARROW NEWS & MAIL, LTD. Furness and district year book and d. Barrow, [1932].   5

1/789   BLACKBURN & DISTRICT INCORPORATED CHAMBER OF COMMERCE. Annual report [and list of members]. Blackburn, 1933.   1

1/790   COLLINSON, RICHARD, LTD., (comp.). Manchester Royal Exchange: d. and guide. Manch., [1932].   1

1/791   COPE, E. F., & CO. Liverpool and district d. and buyers' guide. Walsall, 1932.   17

1/792   GENERAL POST OFFICE. [Telephone d. for] Manchester and south-east Lancashire district (including Rochdale). June and December, 1932.   1

1/793   KELLY'S DIRECTORIES, LTD. Gore's D. of Liverpool and its environs. 1932.   1

1/794   — Slater's D. of Manchester, Salford and suburbs. 1932.   1,3,15,59,C

1/795   MANCHESTER COAL EXCHANGE. D. Manch., [1932].   1

1/796   OLDHAM & DISTRICT INCORPORATED CHAMBER OF COMMERCE. Annual report [and list of members]. Oldham, [1933].   1

1/797   PRESTON & DISTRICT INCORPORATED CHAMBER OF COMMERCE. Seventeenth annual report, statement of accounts and list of members. Preston, 1933.   1

1/798   TILLOTSONS NEWSPAPERS LTD. Post Office Bolton d. Bolton, 1932.   1,7

1/799   WORRALL, JOHN, LTD. The Lancashire textile industry. Oldham, 1932.   1,9

1/800   BURY & DISTRICT CHAMBER OF COMMERCE. Annual report
and list of members. Bury, 1933.   1

1/801   COPE, E. F., & CO. Bolton and district d. and buyers' guide.
Walsall, 1932.   50

1933

1/802   BARRETT, P., & CO. General and commercial d. of Burnley
and district including Nelson, Colne, Padiham . . . and
adjacent villages and townships. Preston, 1933.   1,9,32

1/803   BARROW NEWS & MAIL, LTD. Furness and district year book
and d. Barrow, [1933].   5

1/804   BLACKBURN & DISTRICT INCORPORATED CHAMBER OF COM-
MERCE. Annual report [and list of members]. Blackburn,
1934.   1

1/805   COLLINSON, RICHARD, LTD., (comp.). Manchester Royal
Exchange: d. and guide. Manch., [1933].   1

1/806   GENERAL POST OFFICE. [Telephone d. for] Manchester and
south-east Lancashire district (including Rochdale). June
and December, 1933.   1

1/807   KELLY'S DIRECTORIES, LTD. Gore's D. of Liverpool and its
environs. 1933.   1,3

1/808   — Slater's D. of Manchester, Salford and suburbs. 1933.
     1,3,15,59,C

1/809   WORRALL, JOHN, LTD. The Lancashire textile industry.
Oldham, 1933.   1

1933–4

1/810   BURY & DISTRICT CHAMBER OF COMMERCE. Annual report
and list of members. Bury, 1934.   1

1/811   COPE, E. F., & CO. Oldham, Rochdale, and district d. and
buyers' guide. Walsall, 1933.   13

1/812   SEED, R., & SONS. Southport and district d. Preston, 1933.
     1,16,45,RO

1/813   TOWN & COUNTY DIRECTORIES, LTD. Blackburn, Burnley,
Preston, Barrow and district trades d. Edinburgh &
Manch., 1933.   9

1934

1/814   BARRETT, P., & CO. General and commercial d. of Blackpool
and the Fylde. Preston, 1934.   1,3

1/815   BARROW NEWS & MAIL, LTD. Furness and district year book
and d. Barrow, [1934].   5

1/816   BLACKBURN & DISTRICT INCORPORATED CHAMBER OF COMMERCE. Annual report [and list of members]. Blackburn, 1935.   1

1/817   COLLINSON, RICHARD, LTD., (comp.). Manchester Royal Exchange: d. and guide. Manch., [1934].   1

1/818   COPE, E. F., & Co. Bolton and district d. and buyers' guide. Walsall, 1934.   7

1/819   GENERAL POST OFFICE. [Telephone d. for] Manchester and south-east Lancashire district (including Rochdale). June and December, 1934.   1

1/820   KELLY'S DIRECTORIES, LTD. D. of Cheshire. 1934.   1,59

1/821   — Gore's D. of Liverpool and its environs. 1934.   1

1/822   — Slater's D. of Manchester, Salford and suburbs. 1934.   1,3,15,59,C

1/823   MANCHESTER COAL EXCHANGE. D. Manch., [1934].   1

1/824   PRESTON & DISTRICT INCORPORATED CHAMBER OF COMMERCE. Nineteenth annual report, statement of accounts and list of members. Preston, 1935.   12

1/825   SHIRES, F. N., LTD. Lancaster, Morecambe and suburban d. Lancaster, [1934].   3,28

1/826   WORRALL, JOHN, LTD. The Lancashire textile industry. Oldham, 1934.   1

1934–5

1/827   BURY & DISTRICT CHAMBER OF COMMERCE. Annual report and list of members. Bury, 1935.   1

1935

1/828   BARRETT, P., & Co. D. of Blackburn, Accrington, Darwen, Clitheroe . . . and adjacent villages and townships. Preston, 1935.   1,3,19

1/829   BARROW NEWS & MAIL, LTD. Furness and district year book and d. Barrow, [1935].   5

1/830   BLACKBURN & DISTRICT INCORPORATED CHAMBER OF COMMERCE. Annual report [and list of members]. Blackburn, 1936.   1

1/831   COLLINSON, RICHARD, LTD., (comp.). Manchester Royal Exchange: d. and guide. Manch., [1935].   1

1/832   COPE, E. F., & Co. Liverpool and district d. and buyers' guide. Walsall, 1935.   17

1/833   — Preston, Blackpool and district d. and buyers' guide. Walsall, 1935.   28

1/834   GENERAL POST OFFICE. [Telephone d. for] Manchester and
         south-east Lancashire district (including Rochdale). June
         and December, 1935.   1

1/835   KELLY'S DIRECTORIES, LTD.   Gore's D. of Liverpool and its
         environs. 1935.   1

1/836   — Slater's D. of Manchester, Salford and suburbs. 1935.
                                                           1,3,15,59,C

1/837   MANCHESTER COAL EXCHANGE. D. Manch., [1935].   1

1/838   TOWN & COUNTY DIRECTORIES, LTD. Manchester, Liverpool
         and district trades' d. Edinburgh, 1935.   31

1/839   WHIPPLE, R. D., SON, & MARTIN, LTD.   The Rochdale
         county borough d. Leeds, 1935.   1,9,13,RO

1/840   WORRALL, JOHN, LTD.   The Lancashire textile industry.
         Oldham, 1935.   1

1935–6

1/841   BURY & DISTRICT CHAMBER OF COMMERCE. Annual report
         and list of members. Bury, 1936.   1

1/842   WHIPPLE, R. D., SON, & MARTIN, LTD.   The Warrington
         county borough and district d. Leeds, 1935.   17

1936

1/843   AUBREY & CO. D. of Cheshire. 1936.   59

1/844   BARRETT, P., & CO. General and commercial d. of Preston
         and district. Preston, 1936.   1,3,12

1/845   BARROW NEWS & MAIL, LTD. The Furness and district year
         book and d. Barrow, [1936].   3,5

1/846   BLACKBURN & DISTRICT INCORPORATED CHAMBER OF COM-
         MERCE. Annual report [and list of members]. Blackburn,
         1937.   1

1/847   COLLINSON, RICHARD, LTD., (comp.).   Manchester Royal
         Exchange: d. and guide. Manch., [1936].   1

1/848   COPE, E. F., & CO. Cheshire d. and buyers' guide. Walsall,
         1936.   59

1/849   EDWARDS & BRYNING, LTD. The Bury county borough d.
         Rochdale, 1936.   1,10

1/850   GENERAL POST OFFICE. [Telephone d. for] Manchester and
         south-east Lancashire district (including Rochdale).
         June and December, 1936.   1

1/851   KELLY'S DIRECTORIES, LTD.   Gore's D. of Liverpool and its
         environs. 1936.   1,45

1/852   — Slater's D. of Manchester, Salford and suburbs. 1936.
                                                        1,15,25,59,C

1/853　MANCHESTER COAL EXCHANGE. D. Manch., [1936].　　1

1/854　PRESTON & DISTRICT INCORPORATED CHAMBER OF COM-
MERCE. Twenty-first annual report, statement of accounts
and list of members. Preston, 1937.　　12

1/855　TOWN & COUNTY DIRECTORIES, LTD. Manchester, Liverpool
and district trades' d. Edinburgh, 1936.　　59

1/856　WORRALL, JOHN, LTD. The Lancashire textile industry.
Oldham, 1936.　　1

1936–7

1/857　BURY & DISTRICT CHAMBER OF COMMERCE. Annual report
and list of members. Bury, 1937.　　1

1/858　SEED, R., & SONS. Southport and district d. Preston, 1936.　　1,16

1/859　TOWN & COUNTY DIRECTORIES, LTD. Blackburn, Burnley,
Preston, Barrow and district trades d., including Blackpool. Edinburgh, 1936.　　3

1937

1/860　BARRETT, P., & CO. D. and topography of Burnley, Colne,
Nelson, Padiham. Preston, 1937.　　3,9,23,32

1/861　BARROW NEWS & MAIL, LTD. The Furness and district year
book and d. Barrow, [1937].　　3,5

1/862　BLACKBURN & DISTRICT INCORPORATED CHAMBER OF COM-
MERCE. Annual report [and list of members]. Blackburn,
1938.　　1

1/863　COLLINSON, RICHARD, LTD., (comp.). Manchester Royal
Exchange: d. and guide. Manch., [1937].　　1

1/864　GENERAL POST OFFICE. [Telephone d. for] Manchester and
south-east Lancashire district (including Rochdale).
June and December, 1937.　　1

1/865　— [Telephone d. for] Warrington. 1937.　　17

1/866　KELLY'S DIRECTORIES, LTD. Gore's D. of Liverpool and its
environs. 1937.　　1,3,45

1/867　— Slater's D. of Manchester, Salford and suburbs. 1937.
1,15,25,45,59,C

1/868　MANCHESTER COAL EXCHANGE. D. Manch., [1937].　　1

1/869　PRESTON & DISTRICT INCORPORATED CHAMBER OF COM-
MERCE. Twenty-second annual report, statement of
accounts and list of members. Preston, 1938.　　12

1/870　WORRALL, JOHN, LTD. The Lancashire textile industry.
Oldham, 1937.　　1,11

1/871   BURY & DISTRICT CHAMBER OF COMMERCE. Annual report
and list of members. Bury, 1938.   1

1/872   TOWN & COUNTY DIRECTORIES, LTD. Blackburn, Burnley,
Preston, Barrow and district trades d., including Blackpool. Edinburgh & Manch., 1938.   28

1938

1/873   AUBREY & CO. Lancashire d. Walsall, 1938.   16

1/874   BARRETT, P., & CO. General and commercial d. of Blackpool and the Fylde. Preston, 1938.   3,44

1/875   BARROW NEWS & MAIL, LTD. The Furness and district year
book and d. Barrow, 1938.   3,5

1/876   BLACKBURN & DISTRICT INCORPORATED CHAMBER OF COM-
MERCE. Annual report [and list of members]. Blackburn,
1939.   1

1/877   COLLINSON, RICHARD, LTD., (comp.).   Manchester Royal
Exchange: d. and guide. Manch., [1938].   1

1/878   COPE, E. F., & CO. Cheshire d. and buyers' guide. Walsall,
1938.   59

1/879   DOUGLAS, OSBORNE & CO., LTD. Rochdale county borough
d. Leeds, [1938].   1,13

1/880   GENERAL POST OFFICE. [Telephone d. for] Manchester and
south-east Lancashire district (including Rochdale).
June and December, 1938.   1

1/881   — [Telephone d. for] Warrington. 1938.   17

1/882   KELLY'S DIRECTORIES, LTD.   Gore's D. of Liverpool and its
environs. 1938.   1,3

1/883   — Slater's D. of Manchester, Salford and suburbs. 1938.
     1,15,59,C

1/884   MANCHESTER COAL EXCHANGE. D. Manch., [1938].   1

1/885   TOWN & COUNTY DIRECTORIES, LTD. Manchester, Liverpool
and district trades' d. Edinburgh, 1938.   59

1/886   TRADES' DIRECTORIES LTD. North-western counties of England trades' d. Manch., 1938.   17
     Warrington section only.

1/887   WORRALL, JOHN, LTD. The Lancashire textile industry.
Oldham, 1938.   1,11,59

1938–9

1/888   BURY & DISTRICT CHAMBER OF COMMERCE. Annual report
and list of members. Bury, 1939.   1

1/889   TOWN & COUNTY DIRECTORIES, LTD. Blackburn, Burnley, Preston, Barrow and district trades' d., including Blackpool. Edinburgh, 1938.   23

1939

1/890   BARRETT, P., & CO. D. of Blackburn, Accrington, Darwen, Clitheroe . . . and adjacent villages and townships. Preston, 1939.   1,3,19

1/891   BARROW NEWS & MAIL, LTD. Furness and district year book and d. Barrow, [1939].   5

1/892   COLLINSON, RICHARD, LTD., (comp.). Manchester Royal Exchange: d. and guide. Manch., [1939].   1

1/893   GENERAL POST OFFICE. Classified (trades and professions) telephone d.: Manchester area, including Rochdale. 1939.   1,C

1/894   — [Telephone d. for] Manchester and south-east Lancashire district (including Rochdale). June and December, 1939.   1

1/895   KELLY'S DIRECTORIES, LTD. D. of Cheshire. 1939.   1,59,C

1/896   — Gore's D. of Liverpool and its environs. 1939.   1,3

1/897   — Slater's D. of Manchester, Salford and suburbs. 1939.   1,3,15,45,59,C

1/898   TRADES' DIRECTORIES LTD. North-western counties of England trades' d. Manch., 1939.   59

1/899   TRAFFORD PARK ESTATES LTD. Information Bureau. D. of firms located on the industrial estate of Trafford Park, Manchester, 1939. Manch., [1939].   25

1/900   WORRALL, JOHN, LTD. The Lancashire textile industry. Oldham, 1939.   1,11

1939–40

1/901   SEED, R., & SONS. Southport and district d. Preston, 1939.   16

1940

1/902   BARRETT, P., & CO. General and commercial d. of Preston and district. Preston, 1940.   1,3,9,12,22

1/903   BLACKBURN & DISTRICT INCORPORATED CHAMBER OF COMMERCE. Annual report [and list of members]. Blackburn, 1941.   6

1/904   COLLINSON, RICHARD, LTD., (comp.). Manchester Royal Exchange: d. and guide. Manch., [1940].   1

1/905   GENERAL POST OFFICE. [Telephone d. for] Manchester area (including Rochdale). July, 1940.   1,C

1/906   KELLY'S DIRECTORIES, LTD.   Gore's D. of Liverpool and its environs. 1940.   1,3,45

1/907   — Slater's D. of Manchester, Salford and suburbs. 1940.   1,3,15,59,C

1/908   TRADES' DIRECTORIES LTD. North-western counties of England trades' d. Manch., 1940.   1

1/909   WORRALL, JOHN LTD.   The Lancashire textile industry. Oldham, 1940.   1,59

1941

1/910   AUBREY & Co. Manchester and district d. Walsall, 1941.   1

1/911   BARRETT, P., & Co. D. and topography of Burnley, Colne, Nelson, Padiham. Preston, 1941.   1,3,9,23,32

1/912   GENERAL POST OFFICE. [Telephone d. for] Manchester area (including Rochdale). July, 1941.   1,C

1/913   KELLY'S DIRECTORIES, LTD.   Gore's D. of Liverpool and its environs. 1941.   1,3,45

1/914   WORRALL, JOHN, LTD.   The Lancashire textile industry. Oldham, 1941.   1,11

1942

1/915   BARRETT, P., & Co. D. of Blackburn, Accrington, Darwen, Clitheroe . . . and adjacent villages and townships. Preston, 1942.   1,3,19

1/916   COLLINSON, RICHARD, LTD., (comp.).   Manchester Royal Exchange: d. and guide. Manch., [1942].   1

1/917   GENERAL POST OFFICE. [Telephone d. for] Manchester area (including Rochdale). July, 1942.   1,C

1/918   KELLY'S DIRECTORIES, LTD. Slater's D. of Manchester, Salford and suburbs. 1942.   1,3,15,45,59,C

1/919   WORRALL, JOHN, LTD.   The Lancashire textile industry. Oldham, 1942.   1

1943

1/920   COLLINSON, RICHARD, LTD., (comp.).   Manchester Royal Exchange: d. and guide. Manch., [1943].   1

1/921   KELLY'S DIRECTORIES, LTD.   Gore's D. of Liverpool and its environs. 1943.   1,3,45

1944

1/922   BARRETT, P., & Co. General and commercial d. of Preston and district. Preston, 1944.   1,3,12,RO

1/923   COLLINSON, RICHARD, LTD., (comp.).   Manchester Royal Exchange: d. and guide. Manch., [1944].   1

1/924   CONNELL & BAILEY, LTD.   Street d. for Stockport. Stockport, [1944].   59

1/925   GENERAL POST OFFICE. [Telephone d. for] Manchester area (including Rochdale). January, 1944.   1

1/926   WORRALL, JOHN, LTD.   The Lancashire textile industry. Oldham, 1944.   1

1945

1/927   BARRETT, P., & CO.   D. and topography of Burnley, Colne, Nelson, Padiham.   Preston, 1945.   1,3,9,23,32

1/928   COLLINSON, RICHARD, LTD., (comp.).   Manchester Royal Exchange: d. and guide. Manch., [1945].   1

1/929   CONNELL & BAILEY, LTD.   Street d. for Stockport. Stockport, [1945].   59

1/930   GENERAL POST OFFICE. [Telephone d. for] Manchester area (including Rochdale). July, 1945.   1

1/931   KELLY'S DIRECTORIES, LTD.   Slater's D. of Manchester, Salford and Stretford and suburbs. 1945.   1,3,15,45,59,C

1/932   WORRALL, JOHN, LTD.   The Lancashire textile industry. Oldham, 1945.   1

1946

1/933   COLLINSON, RICHARD, LTD., (comp.).   Manchester Royal Exchange: d. and guide. Manch., [1946].   1

1/934   GENERAL POST OFFICE. [Telephone d. for] Manchester area (including Rochdale). July, 1946.   1

1/935   KELLY'S DIRECTORIES, LTD.   Gore's D. of Liverpool and its environs. 1946.   1,3,22,45

1/936   TRAFFORD PARK ESTATES LTD. Information Bureau. D. of firms located on the industrial estate of Trafford Park, Manchester. Manch., 1946.   25

1/937   WORRALL, JOHN, LTD.   The Lancashire textile industry. Oldham, 1946.   1

1946–7

1/938   BURY & DISTRICT CHAMBER OF COMMERCE. Annual report and list of members. Bury, 1947.   1

1947

1/939   BARRETT, P., & CO.   D. of Blackburn, Accrington, Darwen, Clitheroe . . . and adjacent villages and townships. Preston, 1947.   1,3,19,RO

1/940   COLLINSON, RICHARD, LTD., (comp.).   Manchester Royal Exchange: d. and guide. Manch., [1947].   1

1/941 GENERAL POST OFFICE. [Telephone d. for] Manchester
area (including Rochdale). September, 1947.   1

1947–8

1/942 BURY & DISTRICT CHAMBER OF COMMERCE. Annual report
and list of members. Bury, 1948.   9

1948

1/943 BARRETT, P., & CO. General and commercial d. of Preston
and district. Preston, 1948.   1,3,5,9,12,22

1/944 COLLINSON, RICHARD, LTD., (comp.). Manchester Royal
Exchange: d. and guide. Manch., [1948].   1

1/945 GENERAL POST OFFICE. Classified (trades and professions)
telephone d.: Manchester area, including Rochdale. 1948.   1,25,C

1/946 — [Telephone d. for] Manchester area (including Rochdale). November, 1948.   1,25

1/947 — [Telephone d. for] Warrington. 1948.   17

1/948 KELLY'S DIRECTORIES, LTD. Slater's D. of Manchester,
Salford and Stretford and suburbs. 1948.   1,3,15,59,C

1/949 TRAFFORD PARK ESTATES LTD. Information Bureau. D. of
firms located on the industrial estate of Trafford Park,
Manchester. Manch., [1948].   1,25

1/950 WORRALL, JOHN, LTD. The Lancashire textile industry.
Oldham, 1948.   1,59,RO

1948–9

1/951 BURY & DISTRICT CHAMBER OF COMMERCE. Annual report
and list of members. Bury, 1949.   1

1/952 TOWN & COUNTY DIRECTORIES, LTD. Manchester, Liverpool and district trades' d. Edinburgh, 1948.   3,17(Warr. only)

1949

1/953 BARRETT, P., & CO. D. and topography of Burnley, Colne,
Nelson, Padiham. Preston, 1949.   1,3,9,28

1/954 COLLINSON, RICHARD, LTD., (comp.). Manchester Royal
Exchange: d. and guide. Manch., [1949].   1

1/955 GENERAL POST OFFICE. [Telephone d. for] Manchester area
(including Rochdale). August, 1949.   1

1/956 — Telephone d.: Warrington and district. 1949.   17

1/957 KELLY'S DIRECTORIES, LTD. Gore's D. of Liverpool and its
environs. 1949.   1,3,45

1/958 MANCHESTER COAL EXCHANGE. D. Manch., [1949].   1

1/959 WORRALL, JOHN, LTD. The Lancashire textile industry.
Oldham, 1949.   1

1/960 BURY & DISTRICT CHAMBER OF COMMERCE. Annual report and list of members. Bury, 1950. 1

1950

1/961 COLLINSON, RICHARD, LTD., (comp.). Manchester Royal Exchange: d. and guide. Manch., [1950]. 1

1/962 GENERAL POST OFFICE. [Telephone d. for] Manchester (including Rochdale). August, 1950. 1

1/963 GROVE PUBLISHING CO. (MANCHESTER) LTD. Ashton-under-Lyne and district trades' and industrial d. Manch., 1950. 1

1/964 MANCHESTER COAL EXCHANGE. D. Manch., [1950]. 1

1/965 OLDHAM & DISTRICT INCORPORATED CHAMBER OF COMMERCE. Annual report [and list of members]. Oldham, 1950. 11

1/966 WORRALL, JOHN, LTD. The Lancashire textile industry. Oldham, 1950. 1,3,59

1950–1

1/967 BARROW NEWS & MAIL, LTD. The Furness and district year book and d. Barrow, [1950]. 3,5

1/968 BURY & DISTRICT CHAMBER OF COMMERCE. Annual report and list of members. Bury, 1951. 1,10

1951

1/969 BARRETT, P. & CO. D. of Blackburn, Accrington, Darwen, Clitheroe . . . and adjacent villages and townships. Preston, 1951. 1,3,19

1/970 COLLINSON, RICHARD, LTD., (comp.). Manchester Royal Exchange: d. and guide. Manch., [1951]. 1

1/971 GENERAL POST OFFICE. Classified (trades and professions) telephone d.: Blackpool and Preston, 1951. 12

1/972 — Classified (trades and professions) telephone d.: Manchester area, including Rochdale. 1951. 1,25,C

1/973 — [Telephone d. for] Manchester (including Rochdale). August, 1951. C

1/974 KELLY'S DIRECTORIES, LTD. Slater's D. of Manchester, Salford and Stretford and suburbs. 1951. 1,3,15,59,C

1/975 MANCHESTER COAL EXCHANGE. D. Manch., [1951]. 1

1/976 PROVINCIAL SPORTS PUBLICATIONS. D. of Southport and district, including Banks, Formby, and Freshfield. Southport, [1951]. 1,3,16,45

1/977 WORRALL, JOHN, LTD. The Lancashire textile industry. Oldham, 1951. 1,59

1/978   BURY & DISTRICT CHAMBER OF COMMERCE. Annual report
and list of members. Bury, 1952.   10

1/979   KENT SERVICE LTD. Warrington and district d. [1951].   1

1/980   TOWN & COUNTY DIRECTORIES, LTD. Manchester, Liverpool and district trades' d. Edinburgh, 1951.   17
    Warrington section only.

1952

1/981   BARRETT'S PUBLICATIONS LTD. General and commercial d.
of Preston and district. 1952.   1,3,7,9,12

1/982   BARROW NEWS & MAIL, LTD. The Furness and district year
book and d. Barrow, [1952].   3,5

1/983   COLLINSON, RICHARD, LTD., (comp.). Manchester Royal
Exchange: d. and guide. Manch., [1952].   1

1/984   GENERAL POST OFFICE. [Telephone d. for] Manchester
area (including Rochdale). November, 1952.   1,C

1/985   KELLY'S DIRECTORIES, LTD. Gore's D. of Liverpool and its
environs. 1952.   1,3,45

1/986   KENT SERVICE LTD. Wigan and district d. 1952.   1

1/987   MANCHESTER COAL EXCHANGE. D. Manch., [1951].   1

1/988   SHAW & CROMPTON TRADERS' ASSOCIATION. Golden Jubilee
d. of Crompton. Shaw, [1952].   1

1/989   TRAFFORD PARK ESTATES LTD. Information Bureau. D. of
firms located on the industrial estate of Trafford Park
and its vicinity. Manch., 1952.   1,15

1/990   WORRALL, JOHN, LTD. The Lancashire textile industry.
Oldham, 1952.   1

1952–3

1/991   BARRETT'S PUBLICATIONS LTD. General and commercial d.
of Blackpool and the Fylde. 1952.   3

1/992   BURY & DISTRICT CHAMBER OF COMMERCE. Annual report
and list of members. Bury, 1953.   10

1/993   KENT SERVICE LTD. Bury d. 1952.   1,10

1953

1/994   BARRETT'S PUBLICATIONS LTD. D. and topography of Burnley, Colne, Nelson, Padiham. Blackpool, 1953.   1,3,9

1/995   COLLINSON, RICHARD, LTD., (comp.). Manchester Royal
Exchange: d. and guide. Manch., [1953].   1

1/996   GENERAL POST OFFICE. Classified (trades and professions)
telephone d.: Manchester area, including Rochdale, 1953.   1,C

1/997 — [Telephone d. for] Manchester area (including Rochdale). November, 1953. 1,C

1/998 HAMILTON PUBLICATIONS. Burnley, Nelson, Colne, Padiham, Trawden and Barrowford street and trades d. Burnley, 1953. 23

1/999 KENT SERVICE LTD. Wigan and district d. 1953. 18

1/1000 MANCHESTER COAL EXCHANGE. D. Manch., 1953. 1

1/1001 WORRALL, JOHN, LTD. The Lancashire textile industry. Oldham, 1953. 1,5,59

1953–4

1/1002 BURY & DISTRICT CHAMBER OF COMMERCE. Annual report and list of members. Bury, 1954. 10

1/1003 MANCHESTER CHAMBER OF COMMERCE. D. Manch., [1953]. 1

1/1004 TOWN & COUNTY DIRECTORIES, LTD. Manchester, Liverpool and district trades' d. Edinburgh, 1953. 3,17(Warr. only)

1954

1/1005 BARRETT'S PUBLICATIONS LTD. The Stockport county borough d. Blackpool, 1954. 1,59

1/1006 COLLINSON, RICHARD, LTD., (comp.). Manchester Royal Exchange: d. and guide. Manch., [1954]. 1,5

1/1007 GENERAL POST OFFICE. Classified telephone d.: Blackpool and Preston, 1954. 12

1/1008 — [Telephone d. for] Manchester area (including Rochdale). October, 1954. C

1/1009 KELLY'S DIRECTORIES, LTD. Slater's D. of Manchester, Salford and Stretford and suburbs. 1954. 1,3,15,45,59,C

1/1010 KENT SERVICE LTD. Wigan and district d. 1954. 1

1/1011 MANCHESTER COAL EXCHANGE. D. Manch., [1954]. 1

1/1012 OLDHAM & DISTRICT INCORPORATED CHAMBER OF COMMERCE. Annual report [and list of members]. Oldham, 1954. 11

1/1014 WORRALL, JOHN, LTD. The Lancashire textile industry. Oldham, 1954. 1,3,11

1954–5

1/1015 BURY & DISTRICT CHAMBER OF COMMERCE. Annual report and list of members. Bury, 1955. 10

1/1016 KENT SERVICE LTD. Rochdale d., including Milnrow, Littleborough, and Wardle. [1954]. 1,13

1/1017 TOWN & COUNTY DIRECTORIES, LTD. Blackburn, Burnley, Preston, Barrow and district trades' d., including Blackpool. Edinburgh, 1954.   33

1/1018 — Manchester, Liverpool and district trades' d. Edinburgh & Manch., 1954.   1,17,25,59

1/1019 TRADES' DIRECTORIES LTD. North-western counties of England trades' d. Manch., 1955.   3,17(Warr. only),28,59

1955

1/1020 COLLINSON, RICHARD, LTD., (comp.).   Manchester Royal Exchange: d. and guide. Manch., [1955].   1

1/1021 GENERAL POST OFFICE. Classified (trades and professions) telephone d.: Manchester area, including Rochdale. 1955.   1,C

1/1022 — [Telephone d. for] Manchester area (including Rochdale. November, 1955.   1,C

1/1023 KELLY'S DIRECTORIES, LTD.   Gore's D. of Liverpool and its environs. 1955.   1,45

1/1024 KENT SERVICE LTD. Bolton d. [1955].   1,3,7,43

1/1025 MANCHESTER COAL EXCHANGE.   D.   Manch., [1955].   1

1/1026 PROVINCIAL SPORTS PUBLICATIONS.   D. of Southport and district, including Banks, Formby and Freshfield. 1955.   3,16,45

1/1027 TRAFFORD PARK ESTATES, LTD. Information Bureau. D. of firms located on the industrial estate of Trafford Park and its vicinity. Manch., 1955.   25

1/1028 WORRALL, JOHN, LTD.   The Lancashire textile industry. Oldham, 1955.   1,11,59

1955–6

1/1029 BURY & DISTRICT CHAMBER OF COMMERCE. Annual report and list of members. Bury, 1956.   10

1/1030 MANCHESTER CHAMBER OF COMMERCE. D. Manch., [1955].   1

1/1031 TOWN & COUNTY DIRECTORIES, LTD. Blackburn, Burnley, Preston, Barrow and district trades' d., including Blackpool. Edinburgh, 1955.   3,23

1/1032 — Manchester, Liverpool and district trades' d. Edinburgh, 1955.   59

1/1033 TRADES' DIRECTORIES LTD. North-western counties of England trades' d. Manch., 1955.   28,59

1956

1/1034 COLLINSON, RICHARD, LTD., (comp.).   Manchester Royal Exchange: d. and guide. Manch., [1956].   1

1/1035 GENERAL POST OFFICE. Classified telephone d.: Blackpool
and Preston, 1956. 12

1/1036 — [Telephone d. for] Manchester area (including Rochdale).
December, 1956. 1,C

1/1037 MANCHESTER COAL EXCHANGE. D. Manch., [1956]. 1

1/1038 OLDHAM & DISTRICT INCORPORATED CHAMBER OF COM-
MERCE. Annual report [and list of members]. Oldham,
1956. 11

1/1039 WORRALL, JOHN, LTD. The Lancashire textile industry.
Oldham, 1956. 1,11,59

1956–7

1/1040 BURY & DISTRICT CHAMBER OF COMMERCE. Annual report
and list of members. Bury, 1957. 10

1/1041 COUNTY PUBLICITY, LTD. Lancaster and district d. Carlisle,
[1957]. 1,28

1/1042 TOWN & COUNTY DIRECTORIES, LTD. Manchester, Liverpool and district trades' d. Edinburgh, 1956. 3

1957

1/1043 BARRETT'S PUBLICATIONS LTD. Bury county borough d.
St. Annes-on-Sea, 1957. 10

1/1044 CHAMBERS TRADES REGISTERS & DIRECTORIES, LTD. Trades
register of Manchester, Liverpool and districts. 1957. 59

1/1045 COLLINSON, RICHARD, LTD., (comp.). Manchester Royal
Exchange: d. and guide. Manch., [1957]. 1

1/1046 GENERAL POST OFFICE. Classified (trades and professions)
telephone d.: Manchester area, including Rochdale. 1957. 25,C

1/1047 — Warrington exchange telephone numbers. 1957. 17
Published before the automatic exchange came into use, to assist
people in finding the number corresponding to the 5-digit number
shown in the d.

1/1048 KELLY'S DIRECTORIES, LTD. Slater's D. of Manchester,
Salford and Stretford and suburbs. 1957. 1,15,25,59,C

1/1049 MANCHESTER CHAMBER OF COMMERCE. D. Manch., [1957]. 1

1/1050 MANCHESTER COAL EXCHANGE. D. Manch., [1957]. 1

1/1051 OLDHAM & DISTRICT INCORPORATED CHAMBER OF COM-
MERCE. Annual report [and list of members]. Oldham,
1957. 11

1/1052 WORRALL, JOHN, LTD. The Lancashire textile industry.
Oldham, 1957. 1,3,11

INDEXES

(1) NATIONAL AND COUNTY DIRECTORIES

(2) DIRECTORIES COVERING LARGE AREAS WITHIN THE COUNTY

(3) DIRECTORIES OF INDIVIDUAL LOCALITIES

(4) PUBLISHERS

INDEXES

The following references are the dates of the directories with the progressive numbers as shown in the Chronological List.

NATIONAL AND COUNTY DIRECTORIES

1781(14); 1787(16); 1789(20); 1790–8(22); 1805–06–07(32); 1809–10–11(35); 1814–15(41); 1816–17(43,44); 1818(48); 1818–19–20(49,50); 1819–20(51); 1822–3(57); 1824–5(59); 1828(65); 1828–9(67); 1830–1(76); 1834(84); 1844(106); 1848 (121); 1851(134,135); 1854–5(146); 1856 (150); 1858(155,159); 1861(166); 1864 (172); 1865(181); 1869(191,192); 1871–2 (205); 1873(210); 1876(224); 1879 (237); 1881(246,251); 1884(269); 1887 (285,290,298); 1889(318); 1890(329); 1891(336,342,346); 1892(355,357); 1895 (387); 1897(408); 1898(416,418); 1899 (433); 1900(450); 1901(456); 1903(482); 1905(498); 1908(534); 1909(542,546); 1910(557); 1911(569); 1912(580); 1913 (588,593); 1914(603); 1915(615); 1916 (623); 1917(630); 1918(634,637); 1920 (649); 1921(659); 1922(672); 1923(683); 1924(688,693); 1925(706); 1926(716); 1927(727); 1928(740); 1929(753); 1930 (768); 1931(781); 1932(786,799); 1933 (809); 1934(826); 1935(840); 1936(856); 1937(870); 1938(873,887); 1939(898, 900); 1940(908,909); 1941(914); 1942 (919); 1944(926); 1945(932); 1946(937); 1948(950); 1949(959); 1950(966); 1951 (977); 1952(990); 1953(1001); 1954 (1014); 1954–5(1019); 1955(1028); 1955–6(1033); 1956(1039); 1957(1052).

DIRECTORIES COVERING LARGE AREAS

Amounderness 1851(129).

East Lancashire 1868(185,186).

Furness 1829(69); 1876(222); 1882(256); 1886(281); 1896(394); 1897(404); 1898 (412); 1899(424); 1900(439,443); 1901 (458); 1902(466); 1903(475); 1904(486); 1905(497); 1906(507); 1907(518); 1908 (528); 1909(541); 1911(563); 1926(709); 1927(718); 1928(731); 1929(743); 1930 (756); 1931(772); 1932(788); 1933(803); 1934(815); 1935(829); 1936(845); 1937 (861); 1938(875); 1939(891); 1950–1 (967); 1952(982).

Fylde 1880(240); 1886(280); 1929(742); 1934(814); 1938(874); 1952–3(991).

Lonsdale 1849(122); 1851(129); 1876 (222).

Mid-Lancashire 1854(144); 1855(147); 1921(655); 1922(666); 1923(677).

North Lancashire 1865(178); 1866(182); 1868(186).

North-east Lancashire 1875–6(220).

South-east Lancashire 1921(654); 1922 (665); 1923(676); 1924(687); 1925(701); 1926(712); 1927(721); 1928(735); 1929 (747); 1930(762); 1931(775); 1932(792); 1933(806); 1934(819); 1935(834); 1936 (850); 1937(864); 1938(880); 1939(894). For subsequent telephone directories for this area, see under General Post Office, Manchester area, in Index of Publishers.

DIRECTORIES OF INDIVIDUAL LOCALITIES

Instead of limiting this index to those localities indicated in the main entries or by annotation, an attempt has been made to offer a more comprehensive guide to the contents of the directories included in the foregoing chronological list. In some degree, this has been achieved by adding a small superior letter after the names of places included in directories covering larger areas which stood out as qualifying for this treatment. The key to the superior letter is:

- *a*　Kelly's (Slater's) Manchester directories (current);
- *b*　Kelly's (Slater's) Manchester directories to 1935;
- *c*　Kelly's (Slater's) Manchester directories to 1940;
- *d*　Kelly's (Slater's) Manchester directories to 1942;
- *e*　Kelly's (Gore's) Liverpool directories;
- *f*　Barrett's Blackburn and district directories;
- *g*　Barrett's Preston and district directories;
- *h*　Tillotson's Bolton and district directories;
- *i*　Barrett's Burnley and district directories;
- *j*　Barrett's Blackpool and the Fylde directories;
- *k*　Seed's Wigan and district directories;
- *m*　Kelly's Lancashire directories.

By referring to the index of publishers the appropriate dates of publication and progressive numbers will be easily traced.

Abram *m*　1885(276); 1909(547).

Accrington *f m*　1818(48);　1845(110); 1864–5(176); 1874(213,214); 1875(220); 1878(231);　1879(233);　1881(244);　1882 (254);　1883(259);　1885(271);　1888(302); 1891(332);　1894(367);　1897(402);　1900 (437); 1903(472A); 1906(502); 1909(537); 1912(570);　1915(607);　1925(696);　1930 (755); 1935(828); 1939(890); 1942(915); 1947(939); 1951(969).

Aigburth *e*

Ainsdale *e*　1894–5(375);　1900(448);　1908–09(536); 1914–15(606).

Ainsworth *h*　1881(243); 1885(270).

Aintree *e*

Allerton *e*

Altham *f i m*

Anfield *e*

Ansdell *j m*

Appley Bridge *k m* 1909(547).

Ashton-in-Makerfield *k m* 1885(276); 1909 (547).

Ashton-on-Ribble *f m*　1869(189).

Ashton-under-Lyne *m*　1814–15(41); 1816–17(44);　1818–19–20(49,50);　1845(111); 1853(142);　1871(202);　1874(216);　1884 (268); 1888(308); 1950(963).

Aspull *m*　1885(276).

Astley *m*　1885(275).

Atherton *m*　1885(275).

Audenshaw *c*

Bacup *m*　1787(16);　1789(20);　1816–17 (43);　1845(112,113);　1873(211);　1876 (220); 1879(235).

Baguley *a*

Banks *m*　1894(375);　1900(448);　1908–09 (536); 1951(976); 1955(1026).

Barlow Moor *a*

Barnes Green *a*

Barnfield *d*

Barrow-in-Furness *m*　1871(199);　1876 (222); 1882(256); 1886(281); 1896(394); 1897(404);　1898(412);　1899(424);　1900 (439,443,447);　1901(458);　1902(466); 1903(475);　1904(486);　1905(493,497); 1906(503,507); 1907(514,518);　1908(525, 528);　1909(538,541);　1910(549);　1911 (561); 1912(571); 1913(583); 1914 (595); 1915(608);　1916(616);　1917(625);　1918 (631);　1920(643);　1922(661);　1924(684); 1925(697);　1926(709);　1927(718);　1928 (731); 1929(743); 1930(756); 1930–1(771); 1931(772); 1931–2(785); 1932(788); 1933 (803);　1933–4(813);　1934(815);　1935 (829); 1936(845); 1936–7(859); 1937(861); 1937–8(872);　1938(875);　1938–9(889); 1939(891);　1950–1(967);　1952(982); 1954–5(1017); 1955–6(1031).

Barrowford *i m*　1930(761); 1953(998).

Barton-on-Irwell^d 1828–9(67); 1887(295); 1896(397); 1898(415); 1899(428); 1900 (445); 1902(469); 1903(479); 1904(490).

Besses o' th' Barn^d

Billinge^m 1885(276).

Birkdale^m 1866(182);   1868(184);   1876 (221);   1881(245);   1882–3(258);   1883–4 (266); 1886(283); 1887(292); 1887–8(299); 1890(330);   1892(356);   1893(363);   1894 (372);   1894–5(375);   1895(382);   1896–7 (400);   1900(448);   1900–01(451);   1904 (488);   1906(511);   1908–09(536);   1910–11 (559);   1912–13(581);   1914–15(605,606); 1920–1(650);   1924–5(694,695);   1927–8 (729); 1930–1(770).

Bispham$^{j\ m}$

Blackburn$^{f\ m}$ 1787(16);   1789(20);   1805– 06–07(32); 1809–10–11(35); 1814–15(41); 1816–17(43,44);   1818(48);   1818–19–20 (50); 1845(110); 1852(139); 1864–5(176); 1868(185);   1870–1(196);   1874(213,214); 1875(220);   1878(231);   1879(233);   1881 (244);   1882(254);   1883(259);   1885(271); 1887(284);   1888(302,303);   1889(312); 1890(322); 1891(332,333,335); 1892(349); 1893(360);   1894(367,368);   1895(378); 1896(391);   1897(402,403);   1898(410); 1899(420);   1900(437,438);   1901(453); 1902(462);   1903(472A,473);   1904(484); 1905(494);   1906(502,504);   1907(515); 1908(526);   1909(537,539);   1910(550); 1911(562);   1912(570,572);   1913(584); 1914(596);   1915(607,609);   1916(617); 1917(626);   1918(632);   1919(638);   1920 (644);   1921(651,655);   1922(662,666); 1923(674,677); 1924(685); 1925(696,698); 1926(710);   1927(719);   1928(732);   1929 (744);   1930(755,757);   1931(773);   1932 (789);1933(804); 1933–4(813); 1934(816); 1935(828,830);   1936(846);   1936–7(859); 1937(862);   1937–8(872);   1938(876); 1938–9(889); 1939(890); 1940(903); 1942 (915);   1947(939);   1951(969);   1954–5 (1017); 1955–6(1031).

Blackley^a

Blacko$^{i\ m}$

Blackpool$^{j\ m}$ 1831(77);   1857(151);   1858 (157A);   1859(162);   1866(182A);   1871 (200); 1882(255); 1885(272); 1889(311); 1892(348); 1895(377); 1898(409); 1900 (440); 1901(452); 1904(483); 1907(513); 1910(548);   1929(742,746);   1931(774); 1934(814);   1935(833);   1936–7(859); 1937–8(872);   1938(874);   1938–9(889); 1951(971);   1952–3(991);   1954(1007); 1954–5(1017); 1955–6(1031); 1956(1035).

Blackrod$^{h\ m}$ 1885(276).

Blowick^m 1894–5(375); 1900(448); 1908– 09(536).

Blundellsands^e 1894–5(375);   1913(592); 1925(705); 1929(752).

Boggart Hole Clough^a

Bolton$^{h\ m}$ 1787(16);   1789(20);   1793(22); 1805–06–07(32);   1809–10–11(35);   1814– 15(41);   1816–17(43,44); 1818(48); 1818– 19–20(50);   1824–5(59);   1829(71);   1834 (84); 1845(110,112); 1853(142,143); 1861 (164);   1870–1(197);   1871(201);   1874 (212); 1876–7(228); 1881(243); 1885(270); 1887(296); 1888(307); 1889(317); 1890–1 (331); 1892(350); 1892–3(358); 1894(374); 1894–5(376);   1895(388);   1896–8(401); 1899–1901(436); 1900(441,449); 1902–04 (472);   1907(522);   1911(568);   1921(653, 655); 1922(664,666,671); 1923(677); 1925 (700); 1927(726); 1928(734); 1930(760); 1932(798); 1932–3(801); 1934(818); 1955 (1024).

Bolton-le-Sands^m 1899(430).

Boothstown^d

Bootle^e 1870(194);   1915(613);   1922 (667); 1923(679); 1924(689); 1925(702); 1926(713);   1927(722);   1928(737);   1929 (748);   1930(763);   1931(776);   1932(793); 1933(807);   1934(821) ;   1935(835);   1936 (851); 1937(866); 1938(882); 1939(896); 1940(906); 1941(913); 1943(921); 1946 (935);   1949(957);   1952(985);   1955 (1023).

Bradshaw^h

Brierfield$^{i\ m}$

Burnage^a see also Manchester districts.

Burnley$^{i\ m}$ 1787(16);   1789(20);   1793 (22);   1814–15(41);   1816–17(43,44); 1818–19–20(49,50); 1845(110,112); 1876 (220); 1879(233,234); 1883(260); 1890 (321); 1893(359); 1896(390); 1899(419); 1902(461); 1905(492); 1908(524); 1911 (560);   1914(594);   1923(673);   1927–8 (728); 1933(802); 1933–4(813); 1936–7 (859); 1937(860); 1937–8(872); 1938–9 (889); 1941(911); 1945(927); 1949(953); 1953(994,998);   1954–5(1017);   1955–6 (1031).

Bury^m 1787(16);   1789(20);   1793(22); 1809–10–11(35); 1814–15(41); 1816–17 (43,44);   1818–19–20(49,50);   1845(110, 112);   1850(126);   1853(142,143);   1861 (164); 1871(201); 1876(220); 1880(239); 1883(261); 1885(273); 1888(306); 1888–9 (309);   1899(421);   1905(495);   1906 (510); 1907(516,520); 1908(531); 1909 (544);   1910(555);   1911(566);   1912 (574,576,578);   1913(586,590);   1914 (598); 1915(611); 1916(620); 1929–30 (754); 1930–1(769); 1931–2(782); 1932–3 (800);   1933–4(810);   1934–5(827);

1935–6(841);　1936(849);　1936–7(857);
1937–8(871);　1938–9(888);　1946–7(938);
1947–8(942);　1948–9(951);　1949–50
(960); 1950–1(968); 1951–2(978); 1952–3
(992,993); 1953–4(1002); 1954–5(1015);
1955–6(1029); 1956–7(1040); 1957(1043).

Calderstones *e*

Carnforth *m*　1886(279);　1899(430).

Cartmel *m*　1793(22);　1816–17(43);　1829
(69);　1876(222);　1882(256);　1900(439);
1911(563).

Caton *m*　1899(430).

Chadderton *m*　1891(345).

Chatburn *f m*

Childwall *e*

Chorley *g m*　　1793(22);　　1814–15(41);
1816–17(43,44);　1818(48);　1818–19–20
(50);　1835(86);　1851(128);　1861(164);
1872(207,209);　　1874(213,214);　　1875
(220);　1889–90(319);　1895(380).

Chorlton-cum-Hardy *a*　see also Manchester districts.

Chowbent *m*　1816–17(43).

Church *f m*　1818(48);　1864–5(176).

Churchtown *m*　1894–5(375);　1900(448);
1908–09(536).

Clayton-le-Moors *f m*

Cleveleys *j m*

Clifton *d m*　1828–9(67).

Clitheroe *f m*　1793(22);　1818(48);　1876
(220);　1878(231);　1881(244);　1882(254);
1883(259);　1885(271);　1888(302);　1891
(332);　1894(367);　1897(402);　1900
(437);　1903(472A);　1906(502);　1909(537);
1912(570);　1915(607);　1925(696);　1930
(755);　1935(828);　1939(890);　1942(915);
1947(939);　1951(969).

Cliviger *i m*

Colne *m*　1814–15(41);　　1816–17(43,44);
1818–19–20(49,50); 1876(220); 1879(233,
234);　1883(260);　1890(321);　1893(359);
1896(390);　1899(419);　1902(461);　1905
(492);　1908(524);　1911(560);　1914(594);
1923(673);　1927–8(728);　1930(759,761);
1933(802);　1937(860);　1941(911);　1945
(927);　1949(953);　1953(994,998).

Crompton *m*　1952(988).

Crosby *e* (includes Great Crosby and
Little Crosby) 1894–5(375); 1913(592);
1925(705); 1929(752).

Crossens *m*　1894–5(375);　1900(448);
1908–09(536).

Croxteth *e m*

Crumpsall *a*

Culcheth *m*　(nr. Leigh)　1885(275).

Darwen *f m*　1818(48);　1845(110);　1861
(164);　　1870–1(196);　　1874(213,214);
1875(220);　1878(231);　1879(233);　1881
(244);　1882(254);　1883(259);　1885(271);
1888(302);　1891(332);　1894(367);　1897
(402);　1900(437);　1903(472A);　1906(502);
1909(537);　1912(570);　1915(607);　1925
(696);　1930(755);　1935(828);　1939(890);
1942(915);　1947(939);　1951(969).

Davyhulme *d*

Denton *c*

Didsbury *a*　see also Manchester districts.

Dinckley *f m*

Dingle *e*

Downham *f m*

Droylsden *c*

Earlestown *m*　1876(227);　　1883–4(265);
1891(339);　1894–5(385).

Eccles *d m*　1828–9(67);　　1887(291,295);
1888(305);　1891(341);　1896(397);　1898
(415);　1899(428);　1900(445);　1902(469);
1903(479);　1904(490).

Eccleshill *f m*

Eccleston *j m*

Ellel *m*　1899(430).

Elswick *j m*

Everton *e*　1830(73).

Failsworth *c*

Fairfield *e*　(nr. Liverpool).

Fairfield *c*　(nr. Manchester).

Fairhaven *j m*

Fallowfield *a*　see also Manchester districts.

Farnworth *h m*　(nr. Bolton)　1871(201);
1874(212);　1881(243);　1885(270);　1892
(350).

Fazakerley *e*

Fleetwood *j m*　　1857(151);　　1900(440);
1924(688).

Flixton *d*

Formby *m*　1894–5(375);　1908–09(536);
1951(976);　1955(1026).

Foulridge *i m*

Freckleton *j m*

Freshfield　see Formby.

Fulwood *m*　1869(189).

Garstang *j m*　　1794(22);　　1816–17(43);
1899(430).

Garston *e m*

Gathurst *k m*　1909(547).

Golborne *m*　1885(276).

Great Harwood *f m*

Habergham Eaves *i m*

Haigh *k m*　1909(547).

69

Hapton [i] [m]

Haslingden [m] 1787(16); 1789(20); 1816–17(43); 1876(220); 1879(235).

Haughton [c]

Hawkeshead [m] 1794(22).

Heaton Chapel [b] [m]

Heaton Mersey [b] [m]

Heaton Moor [b] [m]

Heaton Norris [m] 1872(208); 1887–8(300).

Heaton Park [d]

Heysham [m] 1899(430).

Heywood [m] 1845(112,113); 1871(201); 1876(220); 1880(239); 1883(261); 1888(306); 1888–9(310).

Hightown [m] (nr. Formby) 1894–5(375); 1913(592); 1925(705); 1929(752).

Hindley [k] [m] 1885(276); 1908(533); 1909(547).

Hollins [d]

Hollinwood [m] 1884(268); 1891(345).

Horwich [h] [m] 1885(270); 1892(350).

Hulme [a]

Huncoat [f] [m]

Huyton-with-Roby [e]

Ightenhill [i] [m]

Ince [k] [m] 1885(276); 1890(324); 1909(547).

Ince Blundell [e] [m] 1913(592); 1925(705); 1929(752).

Irlam [m] 1828–9(67).

Irlams o' th' Height [a]

Kearsley [h] [m] 1874(212); 1881(243); 1885(270).

Kenyon [m] 1885(275).

Kirkby [e]

Kirkdale [e]

Kirkham [g] [j] [m] 1787(16); 1789(20); 1816–17(43).

Knotty Ash [e]

Knowsley [e] [m]

Ladybarn [a]

Lancaster [m] 1684(1); 1787(16); 1789(20); 1794(22); 1805–06–07(32); 1809–10–11(35); 1814–15(41); 1816–17(43,44); 1818–19–20(50); 1864(171); 1881(247); 1886(279,280); 1889(316); 1889–90(320); 1896(392); 1899(422,430); 1901(455); 1912(573); 1913(585); 1944(825); 1956–7(1041).

Langho [f] [m]

Lees [m] 1875(219); 1880(242); 1884(268); 1888(308); 1891(345).

Leigh [m] 1787(16); 1789(20); 1794(22); 1816–17(43); 1818(48); 1853(143); 1861(164); 1871(203); 1876(227).

Levenshulme [a] see also Manchester districts.

Leyland [g] [m]

Litherland [e] 1915(613).

Littleborough [m] 1873(211), 1879(235); 1916(618); 1954–5(1016).

Little Hulton [h] [m]

Little Lever [h] [m]

Liverpool 1766(2,3); 1767(4); 1769(5); 1773(10); 1774(11,12); 1777(13); 1787(16); 1789(20); 1790(21); 1794(22); 1796(24); 1800(27); 1803(29); 1805(31); 1805–06(32); 1807(33); 1809–10–11(35); 1810(36); 1813(39); 1814–15(41); 1816–17(43,44); 1818(47); 1818–19–20(50); 1821(54); 1823(58); 1825(61); 1827(63,64); 1829(68); 1832(79); 1834(82); 1835(85); 1837(88,89); 1839(91); 1841(93); 1843(99,100,101); 1844(105); 1845(108); 1846(114); 1847(117); 1849(123); 1851(130); 1852(136); 1853(140); 1854–5(146); 1855(148); 1857(153); 1858(156,159); 1859(161); 1861(166); 1862(167); 1863(169); 1864(172,173); 1865(179); 1867(183); 1868(187); 1870(194,195); 1872(206); 1873(210); 1874(215) ; 1876(223,224); 1879(236); 1880(241); 1881(246,248); 1883(262,263); 1885(274); 1887(285,287, 290); 1889(314); 1890(325,328); 1891(336,337); 1892(352); 1893(361); 1894(370); 1895(379,387); 1896(395); 1897(405); 1898(411,416); 1899(423); 1900(442); 1901(457); 1902(465); 1903(476); 1904(487); 1905(499); 1906(509); 1907(519); 1908(529,533); 1909(543); 1910(553); 1911(565); 1912(577); 1913(589, 592); 1914(600); 1915(612); 1916(621); 1917(628); 1918(635); 1919(639); 1920(646); 1921(656); 1922(667); 1923(679, 682); 1924(689); 1925(702,705); 1926(713); 1927(722); 1928(737); 1929(748, 752); 1930(763); 1931(776,778); 1931–2(784); 1932(791,793); 1933(807); 1934(821); 1935(832,835,838); 1936(851,855); 1937(866); 1938(882,885); 1939(896); 1940(906); 1941(913); 1943(921); 1946(935); 1948–9(952); 1949(957); 1952(985); 1953–4(1004); 1954–5(1018); 1955(1023); 1955–6(1032); 1956–7(1042); 1957(1044).

Longsight [a]

Lunt [e] [m] 1913(592); 1925(705); 1929(752).

Lytham [j] [m] 1830(75); 1831(77); 1857(151); 1900(440).

Maghull [m] 1908(533).

Manchester and Salford 1772(6,7); 1773(8,9); 1781(15); 1787(16); 1788(17,18); 1789(20); 1794(22,23); 1797(25); 1800

(26); 1802(28); 1804(30); 1805–06–07 (32); 1808(34); 1809–10–11(35); 1811 (37,38); 1813(40); 1814–15(41); 1815 (42); 1816–17(43,44); 1817(46); 1818–19–20(49,50); 1819–20(52); 1821–2(56); 1824–5(60); 1828(66); 1829(70,72); 1830(74); 1830–1(76); 1832(80); 1833 (81); 1834(84); 1836(87); 1837(89); 1838(90); 1840(92); 1841(94,95,96); 1843 (101,102,103,104); 1845(109,112,113); 1846(114,115); 1847(116); 1848(118, 120); 1850(127); 1851(132,133,134); 1852(136,137,138); 1853(142); 1854–5 (145,146); 1855(149); 1857(154); 1858 (156,157,158,159); 1861(165,166); 1863 (168,169); 1864(172,175); 1865(180,181); 1868–9(188); 1869(190); 1871–2(204); 1873(210); 1874(218); 1876(224,225); 1877–8(230); 1879(237,238); 1881(246, 249); 1882(257); 1883(264); 1884(267); 1885(277); 1886(282); 1887(285,286,289, 290,291); 1888(305); 1889(315); 1890 (327); 1891(334,336,340,341,342); 1891–2 (347); 1892(354,355); 1893(365); 1893–4 (366); 1894(373); 1895(386,387); 1895–6 (389); 1896(398); 1896–7(399); 1897(407); 1898(416,417); 1899(427,429); 1899–1900(434); 1900(446); 1901(454,460); 1902(463,470); 1903(474,480); 1904 (485,491); 1905(496,501); 1906(505,506, 512); 1907(517,521); 1908(527,532); 1908–09(535); 1909(540,545); 1910(551, 556); 1910–11(558); 1911(564,567); 1912 (575,579); 1913(587,591); 1914(597,601, 602); 1915(610,614); 1916(619,622); 1917 (627,629); 1918(633,636); 1919(640,642); 1920(645,648); 1921(652,654,658); 1922 (663,665,668,669); 1923(675,676,680); 1924(686,687,690,691); 1925(699,701, 703); 1926(711,712,714); 1927(720,721, 723,724); 1928(733,735,738); 1929(745, 747,749,750); 1930(758,762,764,765); 1931(775,777); 1931–2(784); 1932(790, 792,794,795); 1933(805,806,808); 1934 (817,819,822,823), 1935(831,834,836,837, 838); 1936(847,850,852,853,855); 1937 (863,864,867,868); 1938(877,880,883,884, 885); 1939(892,893,894,897,898); 1940 (904,905,907,908); 1941(910,912); 1942 (916,917,918); 1943(920); 1944(923,925); 1945(928,930,931); 1946(933,934); 1947 (940,941); 1948(944,945,946,948); 1948–9 (952); 1949(954,955,958); 1950(961,962, 964); 1951(970,972,973,974,975); 1952 (983,984,987); 1953(995,996,997,1000); 1953–4(1003,1004); 1954(1006,1008,1009, 1011); 1954–5(1018,1019); 1955 (1020,1021,1022,1025); 1955–6(1030,1032, 1033); 1956(1034,1036,1037); 1956–7 (1042); 1957(1044,1045,1046,1048,1049, 1050).

— : Burnage[a] 1887(294); 1895(383); 1898(414); 1900(444); 1902(468); 1903 (478); 1904(489).

— : Chorlton-cum-Hardy[a] 1887(294); 1898(415); 1899(428); 1900(445); 1902 (469); 1903(479); 1904(490).

— : Didsbury[a] 1887(294); 1895(383); 1898(414); 1900(444); 1902(468); 1903 (478); 1904(489).

— : Fallowfield[a] 1887(294); 1895(383); 1898(414); 1900(444); 1902(468); 1903 (478); 1904(489).

— : Levenshulme[a] 1895(383); 1898 (414); 1900(444); 1902(468); 1903(478); 1904(489).

— : Northenden[a] 1887(288).

— : Trafford Park[a] 1939(899); 1946(936); 1948(949); 1952(989); 1955(1027).

— : Withington[a] 1887(294); 1895(383); 1898(414); 1900(444); 1902(468); 1903 (478); 1904(489).

Marshside[m] (nr. Southport) 1900(448); 1908–09(536).

Martinmere[m] 1900(448).

Marton[j m]

Middleton[m] 1818–19–20(49); 1871(202); 1875(219); 1880(242).

Milnrow[m] 1879(235); 1916(618); 1954–5 (1016).

Monton[b] 1828–9(67) ; 1887(295).

Morecambe[m] 1857(151); 1886(279); 1896(392); 1899(422,430); 1901(455); 1934(825).

Mossley[m] 1875(219); 1888(308).

Mossley Hill[e]

Moston[a]

Nelson[m] 1879(233,234); 1883(260); 1890 (321); 1893(359); 1896(390); 1899(419); 1902(461); 1905(492); 1908(524); 1911 (560); 1914(594); 1923(673); 1927–8 (728); 1930(761); 1933(802); 1937(860); 1941(911); 1945(927); 1949(953); 1953 (994,998).

Netherton[e m] 1913(592); 1925(705); 1929(752).

Newburgh[m] 1900(448).

Newchurch-in-Rossendale[m] 1873(211).

New Moston[a]

Newton Heath[a]

Newton-le-Willows[m] 1798(22); 1871 (203); 1876(227); 1908(533).

Norbreck[j m]

Norden[m] 1916(618).

Northenden[a] see also Manchester districts.

Nuthurst ^{a}

Oldham ^{m} 1814–15(41); 1816–17(43,44); 1817(45); 1818–19–20(49,50); 1845(110, 112); 1871(202); 1875(219); 1880(242); 1881–2(252); 1884(268); 1888(304,308); 1890(326); 1891(338,345); 1892(353); 1893(362); 1894(371); 1895(381); 1896 (396); 1897(406); 1898(413); 1899(426); 1901(459); 1924(688); 1926–7(717); 1928–9(741); 1930(767); 1931(779); 1931–2(783); 1932(796); 1933–4(811); 1950(965); 1954(1012); 1956(1038); 1957(1051).

Ormskirk ^{m} 1787(16); 1789(20); 1816–17 (43); 1872(209); 1908(533).

Orrell ^{e} (nr. Bootle).

Orrell $^{k\ m}$ (nr. Wigan) 1885(276); 1909(547); 1915(613).

Osbaldeston $^{f\ m}$

Oswaldtwistle $^{f\ m}$ 1882(254); 1883(259).

Padiham ^{m} 1879(233,234); 1883(260); 1890(321); 1893(359); 1896(390); 1899 (419); 1902(461); 1905(492); 1908(524); 1911(560); 1914(594); 1923(673); 1927–8 (728); 1933(802); 1937(860); 1941 (911); 1945(927); 1949(953); 1953(994, 998).

Parbold $^{k\ m}$ 1900(448); 1909(547).

Patricroft ^{d} 1828–9(67); 1887(295); 1896 (397); 1898(415); 1899(428); 1900(445); 1902(469); 1903(479); 1904(490).

Peel Green ^{d}

Pemberton $^{k\ m}$ 1885(276); 1890(324); 1909(547).

Pendlebury ^{d} 1828–9(67).

Pendleton ^{a}

Penwortham ^{m} 1869(189).

Pilkington ^{m} 1880(239); 1883(261).

Pilling $^{j\ m}$

Pleasington $^{f\ m}$

Poulton $^{j\ m}$ 1816–17(43).

Preesall $^{j\ m}$

Prescot ^{m} 1787(16); 1789(20); 1798(22); 1814–15(41); 1816–17(43,44); 1818–19–20(50); 1871(203); 1908(533).

Preston ^{m} 1787(16); 1789(20); 1805–06–07(32); 1809–10–11(35); 1814–15(41); 1816–17(43,44); 1818(48); 1818–19–20 (50); 1821(55); 1841(98); 1845(110, 111); 1851(128,131); 1853(141); 1865 (178); 1869(189); 1874(214); 1875(220); 1877(229); 1880(240); 1882(255); 1885 (272); 1886(280); 1889(311); 1892(348); 1895(377); 1898(409); 1900(447); 1901 (452); 1904(483); 1907(513); 1910(548); 1913(582); 1917(624); 1919(641); 1920

(647); 1921(655,657); 1922(660,666, 670); 1923(677,681); 1924(692); 1925 (704); 1926(708,715); 1927(725); 1928 (739); 1929(746,751); 1930–1(771); 1931 (774,780); 1931–2(785); 1932(787,797); 1933–4(813); 1934(824); 1935(833); 1936(844,854); 1936–7(859); 1937(869); 1937–8(872); 1938–9(889); 1940(902); 1944(922); 1948(943); 1951(971); 1952 (981); 1954(1007); 1954–5(1017); 1955–6 (1031); 1956(1035).

Prestwich ^{d} 1883(261); 1896–7(399); 1898 (415); 1899(428); 1900(445); 1902(469); 1903(479); 1904(490).

Radcliffe ^{m} 1861(164); 1871(201); 1876 (220); 1880(239); 1883(261); 1888(306); 1888–9(309); 1906(510); 1907(516,520); 1908(531); 1909(544); 1910(555); 1911 (566); 1912(574,578); 1913(586,590); 1914(598); 1915(611); 1916(620).

Rainscough ^{d}

Ramsbottom ^{m} 1861(164); 1871(201); 1880(239); 1883(261); 1888(306).

Rawcliffe $^{j\ m}$

Rawtenstall ^{m} 1873(211).

Read $^{i\ m}$

Reddish $^{b\ m}$

Ribchester ^{m} 1875–6(220).

Rishton $^{f\ m}$

Rivington $^{g\ m}$

Rochdale ^{m} 1787(16); 1789(20); 1798 (22); 1805–06–07(32); 1809–10–11(35); 1814–15(41); 1816–17(43,44); 1818–19–20(49,50); 1820(53); 1845(110,112, 113); 1858(160); 1873(211); 1879(235); 1885(278); 1888–9(310); 1890(323); 1894(369); 1899–1900(435); 1907–08 (523); 1916(618); 1921(654); 1922(665); 1923(676); 1924(687); 1925(701); 1926 (712); 1926–7(717); 1927(721); 1928 (735); 1928–9(741); 1929(747); 1930 (762); 1931(775); 1931–2(783); 1932 (792); 1933(806); 1933–4(811); 1934 (819); 1935(834,839); 1936(850); 1937 (864); 1938(879,880); 1939(893,894); 1940(905); 1941(912); 1942(917); 1944 (925); 1945(930); 1946(934); 1947(941); 1948(945,946); 1949(955); 1950(962); 1951(972,973); 1952(984); 1953(996, 997); 1954(1008); 1954–5(1016); 1955 (1021,1022); 1956(1036); 1957(1046).

Roe Green ^{d}

Rooden Lane ^{d}

Rossall $^{j\ m}$

Royton ^{m} 1875(219); 1880(242); 1884 (268); 1888(308); 1891(345).

Sabden $^{f\ i\ m}$

Saddleworth ^{m} 1871(202); 1875(219); 1880(242); 1884(268); 1888(308); 1891 (345).

St. Annes-on-the-Sea $^{j\ m}$ 1900(440).

St. Helens ^{m} 1818–19–20(50); 1871(198, 203); 1876(227); 1883–4(265); 1887 (293); 1891(339,343); 1895(384,385); 1908(533).

St. Michael-on-Wyre $^{j\ m}$

Salesbury $^{f\ m}$

Salford see Manchester and Salford.

Salwick $^{j\ m}$

Seaforth ^{e} 1913(592); 1925(705); 1929 (752).

Sefton $^{e\ m}$ 1913(592); 1925(705); 1929 (752).

Sharples ^{m} 1874(212).

Shaw ^{m} 1875(219); 1880(242); 1884 (268); 1888(308); 1891(245).

Shevington $^{k\ m}$ 1885(276); 1909(547).

Simonstone $^{i\ m}$

Singleton $^{j\ m}$

Skelmersdale ^{m} 1908(533).

Skerton ^{m} 1899(430).

Southport ^{m} 1826(62); 1831(77); 1832 (78); 1848(119); 1849(124); 1857(151); 1866(182); 1868(184); 1876(221,226); 1881(245); 1882–3(258); 1883–4(266); 1886(283); 1887(292); 1887–8(299); 1890(330); 1892(356); 1893(363); 1894 (372); 1894–5(375); 1895(382); 1896–7 (400); 1899(431); 1900(448); 1900–01 (451); 1902(471); 1904(488); 1906(511); 1908(533); 1908–09(536); 1910–11(559); 1912–13(581); 1914–15(605,606); 1920–1 (650); 1924–5(694,695); 1927–8(729); 1930–1(770); 1933–4(812); 1936–7(858); 1939–40(901); 1951(976); 1955(1026).

Speke $^{e\ m}$

Stalmine $^{j\ m}$

Stand ^{d}

Standish $^{k\ m}$ 1885(276); 1909(547).

Stockport ^{m} 1787(16); 1789(19,20); 1805–06–07(32); 1809–10–11(35); 1814–15(41); 1816–17(43,44); 1818–19–20 (50); 1822–3(57); 1845(111); 1846(115); 1850(125); 1857(152); 1860 (163); 1864(170,174); 1865(177); 1872 (208); 1874(217); 1878(232); 1883(263); 1887(297); 1887–8(300); 1890(328,329); 1891(344); 1892(351); 1893(364); 1895 (383); 1896(393); 1898(414); 1899(425, 427,432); 1900(444); 1902(464,467, 468); 1903(478); 1904(489); 1905(500); 1906(508); 1910(552,554); 1914(599); 1914–15(604); 1923(678); 1928(730,

736); 1934(820); 1936(843,848); 1938 (878); 1939(895); 1944(924); 1945(929); 1954(1005).

Stretford ^{a} 1898(415); 1899(428); 1900 (445); 1902(469); 1903(479); 1904(490); 1945(931); 1948(948); 1951(974); 1954 (1009); 1957(1048).

Swinton ^{d} 1828–9(67).

Thornton $^{j\ m}$ (nr. Blackpool).

Thornton $^{e\ m}$ (nr. Liverpool) 1925(705); 1929(752).

Tockholes $^{f\ m}$

Todmorden ^{m} 1845(112); 1873(211); 1879(235).

Toxteth ^{e}

Trafford Park ^{a} see also Manchester districts.

Trawden $^{i\ m}$ 1953(998).

Turton $^{h\ m}$ 1874(212); 1881(243); 1885 (270).

Tyldesley ^{m} 1876(227).

Ulverston ^{m} 1787(16); 1789(20).

Unsworth ^{d}

Upholland $^{k\ m}$ 1885(276); 1909(547).

Urmston ^{d}

Walkden $^{h\ m}$ 1881(243); 1885(270).

Walton $^{e\ m}$

Walton-le-Dale $^{g\ m}$ 1869(189).

Wardle ^{m} 1916(618); 1954–5(1016).

Warrington ^{m} 1787(16); 1789(20); 1798 (22); 1805–06–07(32); 1809–10–11(35); 1814–15(41); 1816–17(43,44); 1818–19–20(50); 1828–9(67); 1841(97); 1846 (115); 1851(134); 1871(203); 1876(227); 1883–4(265); 1889(313); 1891(339); 1895(385); 1908(530,533); 1935–6(842); 1937(865); 1938(881,886); 1948(947); 1948–9(952); 1949(956); 1951–2(979, 980); 1953–4(1004); 1954–5(1019); 1957 (1047).

Warton $^{j\ m}$

Waterloo ^{e} 1894–5(375); 1913(592); 1925 (705); 1929(752).

Wavertree ^{e}

West Derby ^{e}

Westhoughton $^{h\ m}$ 1881(243); 1885(270).

Westleigh ^{m} 1885(275).

Whalley $^{f\ m}$ 1818(48); 1875–6(220).

Whitefield ^{d} 1906(510); 1907(520); 1908 (531); 1909(544); 1910(555); 1911(566); 1912(578); 1913(590).

Whitworth ^{m} 1916(618).

Widnes [m] 1854–5(146); 1855(147); 1871 (203); 1876(227); 1883–4(265); 1887 (293); 1891(339); 1895(385); 1908(533.)

Wigan [m] 1787(16); 1789(20); 1805–06–07(32); 1809–10–11(35); 1814–15(41); 1816–17(43,44); 1818–19–20(50); 1824–5 (59); 1838(90); 1845(110,111); 1846 (115); 1848(121); 1853(142,143); 1858 (155); 1861(164); 1869(193); 1872 (209); 1876(227); 1881(250); 1882(253); 1885(276); 1887–8(301); 1890(324); 1903(477,481); 1908(533); 1909(547); 1924(688); 1925–6(707); 1952(986); 1953(999); 1954(1010).

Wilpshire [f] [m]

Winstanley [m] 1885(276).

Winton [d] 1887(295).

Withington [a] *see also* Manchester districts.

Withnell [f] [m]

Woolton [e]

Worsley [d] 1828–9(67).

Worsthorne-with-Hurstwood [i] [m]

Worthington [m] 1885(276).

Wrea Green [j] [m]

Wrightington [m] 1885(276).

(775); 1932(792); 1933(806); 1934(819); 1935(834); 1936(850); 1937(864); 1938 (880); 1939(894); 1940(905); 1941(912); 1942(917); 1944(925); 1945(930); 1946 (934); 1947(941); 1948(946); 1949(955); 1950(962); 1951(973); 1952(984); 1953 (997); 1954(1008); 1955(1022); 1956 (1036); 1957(1046). Manchester area (classified trades), 1939(893); 1948(945); 1951(972); 1953(996); 1955(1021). Mid-Lancashire (alphabetical), 1921(655); 1922(666); 1923(677). Warrington (alphabetical), 1937(865); 1938(881); 1948(947); 1949(956).

GILLBANKS, B. H., & CO. Southport, Blackpool, etc., 1857(151).

GILLETT, G. A. Preston, 1869(189).

GLAZEBROOK, T. K. Southport, 1826(62).

GORE, JOHN (John Gore & Son, Johnson Gore, Johnson Gore & Son). Liverpool, 1766(2); 1774(11); 1777(13); 1790(21); 1796(24); 1800(27); 1803(29); 1805(31); 1807(33); 1810(36); 1813(39); 1818(47); 1821(54); 1823(58); 1825(61); 1827(63); 1829(68); 1832(79). See also Shaw, G. T. for reprints of Gore's 1766. 1767, 1769, 1773 and 1774 directories.

GREEN, A., & CO. Liverpool, 1870(194).

GREEN, B. L. Southport, 1868(184).

GROVE PUBLISHING CO. (MANCHESTER), LTD. Ashton-under-Lyne, 1950(963).

HAMILTON PUBLICATIONS. Burnley, etc., 1953(998).

HASLAM & CO. Warrington, 1889(313). Wigan, etc., 1890(324).

HEAP, JOHN. Bury, 1850(126).

HOLDEN, WILLIAM. General, 1805–06–07 (32); 1809–10–11(35); 1816–17(43).

HOLME, EDMOND. Manchester, 1788(17, 18).

HOLMES, W. Furness, 1903(475); 1904 (486); 1905(497); 1906(507); 1907(518); 1908(528); 1909(541).

JOHNSON, ROBERT, & CO. Southport & Birkdale, 1876(221); 1881(245); 1894–5 (375).

KELLY & CO. (Kelly's Directories, Ltd.). Cheshire, 1857(152); 1864(170); 1865 (177); 1878(232); 1892(351); 1896(393); 1902(464); 1906(508); 1910(552); 1914 (599); 1923(678); 1928(736); 1934(820); 1939(895). Lancashire, 1858(155); 1864 (172); 1873(210); 1881(246); 1887(285); 1891(336); 1901(456); 1905(498); 1909 (542); 1913(588); 1918(634); 1924(688). Lancaster, 1864(171). Liverpool, 1858 (156); 1864(172); 1873(210); 1881(246);

1887(285); 1891(336); 1898(411); 1899 (423); 1900(442); 1901(457); 1902(465); 1903(476); 1904(487); 1905(499); 1906 (509); 1907(519); 1908(529); 1909(543); 1910(553); 1911(565); 1912(577); 1913 (589); 1914(600); 1915(612); 1916(621); 1917(628); 1918(635); 1919(639); 1920 (646); 1921(656); 1922(667); 1923(679); 1924(689); 1925(702); 1926(713); 1927 (722); 1928(737); 1929(748); 1930(763); 1931(776); 1932(793); 1933(807); 1934 (821); 1935(835); 1936(851); 1937(866); 1938(882); 1939(896); 1940(906); 1941 (913); 1943(921); 1946(935); 1949(957); 1951(985); 1955(1023). Manchester, 1858(156,157); 1864(172); 1873(210); 1881(246); 1887(285,286); 1891(336).

KENT SERVICE LTD. Bolton, 1955(1024). Bury, 1952–3(993). Rochdale, 1954–5 (1016). Warrington, 1951–2(979). Wigan, 1952(986); 1953(999); 1954(1010).

LEIGH, J. Lancashire, 1818–19–20(49).

LOVE & BARTON. Manchester Exchange, 1847(116); 1848(118).

MacDONALD & MacDONALD. Rochdale, Milnrow, etc., 1879(235).

MACKERETH, H. W. Furness, 1896(394); 1897(404); 1898(412); 1899(424); 1900 (443); 1901(458); 1902(466).

MACKIE & CO., LTD. Warrington, 1908 (530).

MAITLAND, Police Constable. Bury, 1885 (273).

MANNEX, P., & CO. Barrow, 1876(222). Blackburn, 1868(185); 1874(213). Furness and Cartmel, 1882(256). Lancaster, 1881(247). Mid-Lancashire, 1854 (144); 1855(147). North and East Lancashire, 1868(186); 1875–6(220). Preston, 1851(128); 1865(178); 1874(214); 1877 (229); 1880(240). St Helens, 1871(198). Southport, 1866(182). Westmorland, 1849(122); 1851(129).

MAWDSLEY, J. & J. (James Mawdsley, James Mawdsley & Son, J. Mawdsley & Son). Liverpool, 1834(82); 1835(85); 1837(88); 1839(91); 1841(93); 1843(99); 1845(108); 1847(117); 1849(123); 1851 (130); 1853(140); 1855(148); 1857(153); 1859(161); 1862(167); 1864(173); 1865 (179); 1867(183); 1868(187); 1870(195); 1872(206); 1874(215); 1876(223); 1879 (236); 1880(241); 1881(248); 1883(262); 1885(274); 1887(287); 1889(314); 1890 (325); 1891(337); 1892(352); 1893(361); 1894(370); 1895(379); 1896(395); 1897 (405).

MELSOM, R. A. Cheadle & Northenden, 1887(288).

MORRIS & Co. Ashton-under-Lyne, 1874 (216). Cheshire, 1864(174); 1874(217).

MORRIS, ERNEST. Chorley, 1895(380).

MORRIS, J. S. C. Manchester, 1868–9 (188).

NEW CHESHIRE COUNTY NEWS CO., LTD. Stockport, 1899(425); 1902(467); 1905 (500); 1910(554).

NORTH LONSDALE PRINTING CO. Barrow, 1871(199).

OAKEY, HENRY. Preston, 1851(131); 1853 (141).

PARSON, WILLIAM, & WHITE, WILLIAM. Furness, 1829(69).

PICKEN, ANDREW, & SON. Liverpool, 1827 (64).

PIGOT, JAMES (James Pigot & R. & W. Dean, James Pigot & Co., James Pigot & Son, James Pigot & Isaac Slater). Cheshire, 1834(83). General, 1822–3(57); 1828(65); 1828–9(67); 1830–1(76); 1834(84); 1837 (89); 1841(94). Liverpool, 1843(100,101). Manchester & Salford, 1811(38); 1813 (40); 1815(42); 1817(46); 1818–19–20 (50); 1819–20(52); 1821–2(56); 1824–5 (60); 1829(70); 1830(74); 1832(80); 1833 (81); 1836(87); 1838(90); 1840(92); 1841 (95,96); 1843(101,102).

PLATT, R. Wigan, 1903(477).

POORE, J. Southport, 1849(124).

PORTER, FRANK. Bedford-Leigh, 1885 (275). Bootle, 1915(613). Oldham & Stalybridge, 1881–2(252). Wigan, 1885 (275).

PORTER, WILLIAM. Blackpool, 1858 (157A); 1859(162); 1866(182A); 1871 (200).

PROVINCIAL SPORTS PUBLICATIONS. Southport, 1951(976); 1955(1026).

RADCLIFFE TIMES. Radcliffe, 1906(510); 1907(520); 1908(531); 1909(544); 1910 (555); 1911(566);1912(578); 1913(590).

RAFFALD, ELIZABETH. Manchester, 1772 (6,7); 1773(8,9); 1781(15).

ROBERTS, J. Barrow-in-Furness, 1886 (281).

ROBERTSON, J., & CO. Blackburn, 1864–5 (176). Manchester & Salford, 1864(175).

ROBINSON, C. Chorley, 1835(86).

ROBINSON, FRANK. Southport, 1848(119).

ROGERSON, T. Lancashire, 1818(48).

SCHOLES, JOHN. Manchester & Salford, 1794(23); 1797(25).

SEED, R., & SONS. Southport, 1904(488); 1906(511); 1908–09(536); 1910–11(559); 1912–13(581); 1914–15(605); 1924–5 (694); 1927–8(729); 1930–1(770); 1933–4 (812); 1936–7(858); 1939–40(901). Wigan, 1909–10(547); 1925–6(707).

SHAW, G. T., & SHAW, ISABELLA. Liverpool, 1766(3); 1767(4); 1769(5); 1773 (10); 1774(12).

SHIRES, F. M., LTD. Lancaster, Morecambe, 1934(825).

SLATER, ISAAC (Slater's Directory Ltd., Slater's Directory Ltd. & Kelly & Co., Ltd., Slater's Directory Ltd. & Kelly's Directories, Ltd.). Bury, Heywood, 1888 (306). Cheshire, 1869(191); 1883(263); 1890(328,329). Eccles, 1896(397). General, 1846(114); 1848(121); 1852(136). Lancashire, 1851(134,135); 1854–5(146); 1856(150); 1865(181); 1869(191,192); 1871–2(205); 1876(244); 1879(237); 1887 (290); 1891(342); 1895(387); 1898(416). Levenshulme, 1895(383); 1898(414); 1899 (427); 1900(444); 1902(468); 1903(487); 1904(489). Liverpool, 1844(105,106); 1846(114); 1852(136); 1854–5(146); 1858 (159); 1861(166); 1883(263); 1890(328); 1895(387). Manchester, 1843(102,104); 1844(107); 1845(109); 1846(114); 1848 (120); 1850(127); 1851(132,133); 1852 (136,137); 1854–5(146); 1855(149); 1857 (154); 1858(158,159); 1861(165,166); 1863 (168,169); 1865(180); 1869(190,191); 1871–2(204); 1874(218); 1876(225); 1877–8 (230); 1879(238); 1881(249); 1882(257); 1883(264); 1884(267); 1885(277); 1886 (282); 1887(289,290,291); 1888(305); 1889 (315); 1890(327); 1891(340,341); 1892 (354); 1893(365); 1894(373); 1895(386, 387); 1896(398); 1897(407); 1898(417); 1899(429); 1900(446); 1901(460); 1902 (470); 1903(480); 1904(491); 1905(501); 1906(512); 1907(521); 1908(532); 1909 (545); 1910(556); 1911(567); 1912(579); 1913(591); 1914(602); 1915(614); 1916 (622); 1917(629); 1918(636); 1919(642); 1920(648); 1921(658); 1922(668); 1923 (680); 1924(690); 1925(703); 1926(714); 1927(723); 1928(738); 1929(749); 1930 (764); 1931(777); 1932(794); 1933(808); 1934(822); 1935(836); 1936(852); 1937 (867); 1938(883); 1939(897); 1940(907); 1942(918); 1945(931); 1948(948); 1951 (974); 1954(1009); 1957(1048). Prestwich, 1898(415); 1899(428); 1900(445); 1902(469); 1903(479); 1904(490). St. Helens, 1891(343); 1895(384). Southport, 1882–3(258); 1883–4(266); 1886 (283); 1887(292); 1887–8(299); 1890 (330); 1892(356); 1893(363); 1894(372);

1895(382); 1896–7(400); 1900–01(451). Stockport, 1887–8(300); 1891(344); 1893 (364). Warrington, 1883–4(265); 1891 (339); 1895(385).

SOUTHPORT VISITER. Southport, 1920 (650); 1924–5(695).

STEWART, A. Southport, 1876(226).

SUTTON & CO. St. Helens, etc., 1887(293). Wigan, etc., 1887–8(301).

SYERS, ROBERT. Everton, 1830(73).

THOMPSON, H. Southport, 1914–15(606).

THOMPSON, HARGREAVES. Burnage, etc., 1887(294). Eccles, etc., 1887(295).

TILLOTSON & SON (Tillotson & Son Ltd., Tillotsons Newspapers Ltd.). Bolton, 1876–7(228); 1887(296); 1888(307); 1890–1 (331); 1892–3(358); 1894–5(376); 1896–8 (401); 1899–1901(436); 1902–04(472); 1907(522); 1911(568); 1922(671); 1927 (726); 1932(798). Chorley, 1889–90(319).

TOWN & COUNTY DIRECTORIES, LTD. Blackburn, 1933–4(813); 1936–7(859); 1937–8(872); 1938–9(889); 1954–5(1017); 1955–6(1031). Liverpool, 1908(533); 1923 (682); 1935(838); 1936(855); 1938(885); 1948–9(952); 1951–2(980); 1953–4(1004); 1954–5(1018); 1955–6(1032); 1956–7 (1042). Manchester, 1935(838); 1936 (855); 1938(885); 1948–9(952); 1951–2 (980); 1953–4(1004); 1954–5(1018); 1955–6(1032); 1956–7(1042). Preston, 1900 (447); 1930–1(771); 1931–2(785).

TRADES' DIRECTORIES LTD. North Western counties, 1939(898); 1940(908); 1954–5 (1019); 1955–6(1033). Warrington section only, 1938(886); 1954–5(1019).

TULKET, MARMADUKE, pseud., see Whittle, Peter.

TUNNICLIFF, WILLIAM. Lancashire, 1787 (16); 1789(20).

TURNER, JOHN. Rochdale, 1858(160).

UNIVERSAL BRITISH DIRECTORY. 1790–8 (22).

WARDLE, M. Bolton, 1829(71).

WARDLE, M., & BENTHAM. 1814–15(41).

WARDLE, M., & PRATT. 1816–17(44).

WARDLE, M., & WILKINSON, T. Manchester, 1828(66); 1829(72).

WATSON, W., & CO. Lancaster, 1899(430).

WEAVER, THOMAS. Southport, 1899(431); 1900(448); 1902(471).

WELLS & CO. Lancaster, 1889(316); 1889–90(320).

WENTWORTH PUBLISHING CO. Waterloo, 1913(592); 1925(705); 1929(752).

WHELLAN, W., & CO. Bolton, Bury, etc., 1853(143). Manchester, 1852(138); 1853 (142).

WHEWELL, H., & CO. Bolton, 1889(317); 1894(374); 1895(388); 1900(449).

WHIPPLE, R. D., SON & MARTIN, LTD. Rochdale, 1935(839). Warrington, 1935–6 (842).

WHITE, FRANCIS, & CO. Cheshire, 1860 (163).

WHITTLE, PETER. Blackburn, 1852(139). Preston, 1821(55). Southport, 1831(77).

WHITTLE, PETER, & WHITTLE, H. Lytham, 1830(75); Preston, 1841(98).

WIGAN PRINTING CO. Wigan, 1903(481).

WILLIAMS, J. Bolton, 1845(112). Chester, 1846(115). Preston, 1845(110). Rochdale, 1845(113). Stockport, 1845(111).

WOODS, E. B. Stockport, 1887(297); 1899 (432).

WORRALL, JOHN (John Worrall, Ltd.). Blackburn, 1870–1(196). Bolton, 1870–1 (197); 1871(201). Bury, 1871(201). Chorley, 1872(207). Oldham, 1875(219); 1880(242); 1884(268); 1888(308); 1891 (345). Rochdale, 1873(211); 1885(278). Stockport, 1872(208). Warrington, 1871 (203); 1876(227). Wigan, 1869(193); 1872 (209); 1876(227); 1881(250). Cotton spinners and manufacturers', 1881(251); 1884(269); 1887(298); 1889(318); 1891 (346); 1892(357); 1897(408); 1898(418); 1899(433); 1900(450); 1903(482); 1908 (534); 1909(546); 1910(557); 1911(569); 1912(580); 1913(593); 1914(603); 1915 (615); 1916(623); 1917(630); 1918(637); 1920(649); 1921(659); 1922(672); 1923 (683); 1924(693); 1925(706); 1926(716); 1927(727); 1928(740); 1929(753); 1930 (768); from 1931 title is Lancashire textile industry, 1931(781); 1932(799); 1933(809); 1934(826); 1935(840); 1936 (856); 1937(870); 1938(887); 1939(900); 1940(909); 1941(914); 1942(919); 1944 (926); 1945(932); 1946(937); 1948(950); 1949(959); 1950(966); 1951(977); 1952 (990); 1953(1001); 1954(1014); 1955 (1028); 1956(1039); 1957(1052).